# MACBOOK
# Seniors Guide

The Ultimate User-Friendly Guide for Maximizing Your MacBook Potential with Clear Illustrations and Simple Instructions Step By Step

BY

STEVE CARREN

# MACBOOK SENIORS GUIDE © COPYRIGHT 2024

## ALL RIGHTS RESERVED

### STEVE CARREN

# TABLE OF CONTENTS

# INTRODUCTION

N Getting used to a new computer may be challenging, regardless of whether you're moving from an old Mac to a new one, returning to macOS after a long hiatus, or doing anything else.

Apple Inc. is the company that developed and manufactures the MacBook line of laptop computers. This popular brand is well-known for its elegant design, high-quality materials, and compatibility with Apple's macOS operating system. The performance, reliability, and intuitive design of MacBooks are well recognized.

The MacBook Air and MacBook Pro are two of the several MacBook variants. The MacBook Air is a popular choice for everyday use due to its lightweight design, long battery life, and portability. Conversely, professionals and power users seeking more processing power for tasks like graphic design, software development, and video editing are the target market for the MacBook Pro. It offers more powerful hardware alternatives.

A few instances of how seamlessly MacBooks connect with other Apple goods and services include iCloud, iMessage, FaceTime, and Continuity, which enable customers to switch between their MacBook and other Apple devices like iPhones and iPads.

MacBooks are often commended for their functionality, design, and the Apple ecosystem of services and apps. Their committed user base appreciates their sophisticated design, consistent performance, and the easy-to-use macOS interface.

After being available for some time, MacBooks have become one of the most popular laptop brands available. They are well-made, easy to use, and offer some amazing features. So why do people enjoy them so much? More importantly, what makes them better than laptops running Windows?

Here, we'll cover a variety of reasons why we think Apple laptops are better than those manufactured by competitors, covering subjects including ease of use, robustness, and more.

## 1. DESIGN AND SOCIAL IMAGE

Let's face it: The MacBook is fantastic. While Apple has spent years enhancing its brand's social image as elite and inventive, other laptop makers attempt—and sometimes fail—to imitate their sleek design.

Others will probably think you are creative, stylish, and successful if they see you holding a MacBook. Of course, you can be all of those things with any laptop. Unquestionably, however, MacBooks have a certain social cachet that other laptops do not.

## 2. EASY TO BUY

Purchasing a MacBook is easier than purchasing a Windows or Linux computer for two reasons.

There are only two types available: MacBook Air and MacBook Pro, each catering to a different market segment. This short list of options makes it easier for you to choose the ideal MacBook. Compare this to the offerings of other manufacturers, like HP, who provide many monikers for the same laptops.

Secondly, Apple retail outlets are located all over the globe and are manned by knowledgeable staff members who are happy to help you with your purchase. Apple's online store is easy to use and similarly organized. On the other hand, a lot of other laptop manufacturers may have confusing websites or too packed physical locations.

## 3. LONGEVITY AND RESALE VALUE

One of the best things about MacBooks is how well they hold their value over time. Even while many computers might last you a long time—years or longer—only MacBooks will still look good and fetch a fair price after they're used.

Over time, apps get larger in size and computers become slower overall. However, Apple is one of the best companies when it comes to regularly releasing new software updates for out-of-date hardware. This keeps you safe from security threats and lets you continue to update your Mac with new features as it ages.

One possible explanation for MacBooks' high value retention might be their exceptional durability. Typically, a three-year-old MacBook sells for around half of what it cost when new. A three-year-old Windows laptop, though? If fortune favoured you, you may get 25% of the original cost.

## 4. QUALITY AND DURABILITY

Apple laptops are not just constructed with industry-leading hardware and high-quality materials. A Mac may easily last you six years or more if you give it regular, light maintenance. It's sufficient to just take proper care of your Mac.

In this industry, MacBooks are the market leaders despite intense rivalry from many other computer manufacturers. Because of their aluminum unibody structure, they are robust and far more resistant to wear and tear—until you drop and damage them, of course.

In addition, Apple offers a one-year warranty on all products, and repairs may be quickly booked at the nearest Apple Store.

## 5. MACOS AND APPS

Another important selling point for MacBooks is their operating system. MacOS, the operating system that comes pre-installed on MacBooks, is very trustworthy and easy to use. It was designed specifically for Apple products. Novice people think macOS is easier to use than Windows, despite the general perception that it is not user-friendly.

It also comes with a ton of integrated Mac apps that work with anything else you own from Apple. The App Store has more fantastic applications that are perfect for business, play, and creativity.

## 6. THE MAGIC TRACKPAD

The Magic Trackpad is one of the best features of the MacBook. Its trackpad provides a smooth, responsive tracking experience that is unrivaled by any other laptop on the market for a number of reasons.

First of all, the Apple trackpad's base is haptic feedback. As a result, rather than using buttons hidden under its surface, the trackpad uses magnets and motors to sense a click. As a result, users may click anywhere on the trackpad and it will register. Several Windows laptop manufacturers now use this design.

Secondly, there are several built-in trackpad gestures that, when combined with the software, make using your Mac really easy. To activate Mission Control, for example, swipe up or down with four fingers or squeeze to zoom in or out almost anywhere.

Not to mention, the stunning size and comfort of the trackpad make for quick and easy navigation. The majority of laptops from other firms these days have smaller trackpads since their primary attention is on other features.

## 7. THE IMMERSIVE EXPERIENCE

Another thing that sets MacBooks apart from comparable Windows laptops is their greater audio, visual, and typing experiences, which make them a more complete product. For example, everything seems sharper on Macs due to the higher pixel density of their Retina Displays compared to most Windows laptop panels. Such screens are only seen on very costly Windows laptops.

The scissor-switch keyboard is far more comfortable to type on than the keyboards on most Windows laptops because of its key travel and spacing.

Another thing that sets MacBooks apart from comparable Windows laptops is their greater audio, visual, and typing experiences, which make them a more complete product. For example, everything seems sharper on Macs due to the higher pixel density of their Retina Displays compared to most Windows laptop panels. Such screens are only seen on very costly Windows laptops.

The scissor-switch keyboard is far more comfortable to type on than the keyboards on most Windows laptops because of its key travel and spacing.

## 8. THE APPLE ECOSYSTEM

The whole range of products that Apple develops and distributes includes both software and hardware. Nearly all of Apple's products—i.e., the iPhone, iPad, Apple TV, Apple Watch, Mac, iCloud, Apple Music, and so on—are included in the ecosystem.

Consequently, when people speak about the Apple ecosystem, they are really discussing how well these products work together. Thanks to the ecosystem, you can start an activity (like reading an article) on your iPhone and pick up where you left off on your Mac or iPad.

The fact that transitioning between Apple products is so smooth is one of the main reasons MacBooks outperform Windows computers. Although several other laptop makers have attempted to build their own ecosystems, none of them have achieved the same level of success as Apple.

Because of the special advantages of the Apple ecosystem and years of user experience research and development, MacBooks provide a more smooth and integrated experience than rival laptops.

## MACBOOKS VS. OTHER LAPTOPS: MAKE THE RIGHT CHOICE

Selecting a MacBook over other laptop kinds, such Windows or Linux laptops, has several advantages, such as its resilience, market value, style, and social status. Given their ease of purchase and excellent multimedia experience, MacBooks are clearly the best products in their respective sectors.

Choose Wisely Between MacBooks and Other Laptops

Selecting a MacBook over other laptop kinds, such Windows or Linux laptops, has several advantages, such as its resilience, market value, style, and social status. Given their ease of purchase and excellent multimedia experience, MacBooks are clearly the best products in their respective sectors.

However, there are still some issues with MacBooks. Depending on your needs, the MacBook may not be the ideal option for you. One such situation where MacBooks aren't made with gamers in mind is gaming.

# HOW TO PICK THE IDEAL MAC FOR YOU

If you haven't bought a new Mac yet and aren't sure which model to choose, I have some advise for you.

If you require mobility, then you'll choose any model of MacBook. Searching for one that is affordable, lightweight, and small? You will probably want a MacBook Air. Do you need a portable gadget with a larger display or one that is a little bit more powerful? What you need is a MacBook Pro.

If your intention is to leave your Mac on your desk, stay away from the portable options and go for a desktop model. If all you need is a low-cost replacement for a Windows desktop PC and you already own a fantastic HDMI monitor, the Mac mini might be the best choice. If you want a simple all-in-one system with an attractive integrated display, you may also choose an iMac. If you are a power user with really high performance needs (such someone who works with 4K video on a regular basis), you should purchase a Mac Studio.

Before using Universal Control on your Mac, it has to be configured. Please take note that this feature is only supported by macOS Monterey 15.3 or later.

Open System Preferences from the dock icon or the Apple menu.

Go to Displays.

At the bottom of the window, click the Advanced button.

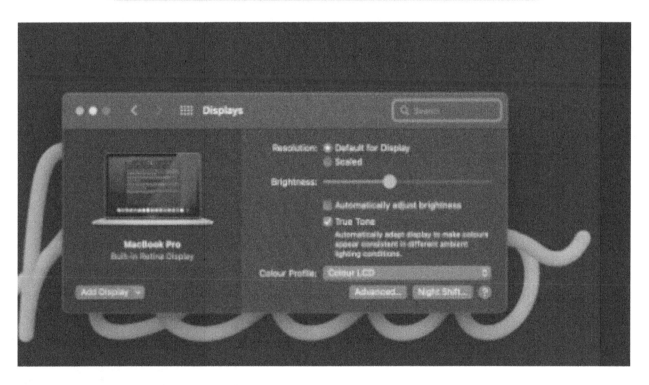

When the new page loads, check the boxes next to each item: Allow the pointer and keyboard to move on any nearby Mac or iPad. Push through the edge of the display to connect to a nearby Mac or iPad, and it will instantly reconnect to any other nearby Mac or iPad.

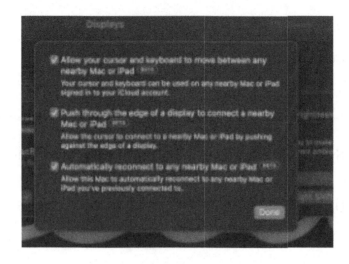

Then, select Done

At this point, your Mac may be used with other devices using Universal Control. You must first setup those devices, however!

## SET UP UNIVERSAL CONTROL ON IPAD

Before using Universal Control on your iPad, it has to be configured. Note that this feature is only supported by iPadOS 15.4 or later.

Go to Settings from the App Library or your home screen.

Navigate to the General menu on the left.

Once you've sorted through the list, choose AirPlay& Handoff.

Once you are on that page, activate the keyboard and cursor options.

You may now utilize Universal Control on your iPad.

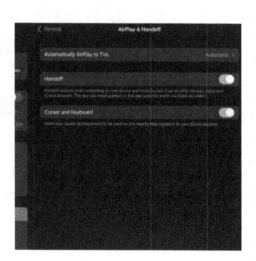

After That?

Now that Universal Control is configured and operational, the fun part can begin!

To utilize Universal Control, your devices need to be in close proximity to one another. If they are further away, you won't be able to follow your keyboard or mouse. You may use Universal Control with up to three Mac and iPad devices, as I said before.

## IS IT POSSIBLE TO USE SIDECAR AND UNIVERSAL CONTROL SIMULTANEOUSLY?

If you connect two devices at the same time, you can really use Universal operate to control one while utilizing Sidecar to use the other as a display. For example, in the setup shown in the procedures below, the iPad Pro is being used with Universal Control, the laptop linked to Sidecar serves as the secondary display, and the main computer is a desktop Mac. It is also feasible to utilize a Mac in addition to two iPads. Here's how to configure it.

- Connect Universal Control to every device in your possession.
- Once Universal Control is setup, you will assign tasks to the devices. You should open the Displays system preference.
- Click to add a display. A drop-down menu lists the various displays along with their respective functionalities. The devices that are mentioned in the Link Keyboard and Mouse section should be used in conjunction with Universal Control. Select the device of your choosing.
- Press Add Display again. Check out the drop-down menu's "Mirror or extend to" section. If you'd like, you may utilize them as additional displays. This collection of iPads and Macs may be used with Sidecar to provide your Mac an additional display. Select the device of your choosing.
- Preference for the system All screens need to be closed.

You should be ready to go. You may change Sidecar and Universal Control assignments and go back to the Displays system choices by clicking and dragging the icons for the displays' layouts at the top of the settings. If you have Sidecar installed, you may switch the iPad's settings from Sidecar to Universal Control by going to the Home screen and tapping the Sidecar app in the Dock.

## SHOULD YOU USE UNIVERSAL CONTROL OR SIDECAR?

Most people will, however, choose one over the other, and you can probably decide for yourself which is ideal for your needs. If you're not persuaded, consider the following examples.:

- You prefer to use iPad apps than Mac ones.
- You don't have a Mac app for the iPad app you have.
- You want to transfer data across devices but don't want to use AirDrop, cloud storage services, or external storage.
- Using two Macs is simpler when one set of input devices is managed.

  When doing hardware management, you must use an other Mac or iPad for administration purposes.

If any of them apply to you, Universal Control should be used. It's a fantastic feature that, although being relatively new, may begin to blur the distinctions between the Mac and the iPad while maintaining the unique qualities of each device.

But if you usually use a Mac and only want to use touch gestures or expand the desktop, Sidebar is the way to go. With all of your software tools, the Mac is usually the main production tool. Completing your work is made much easier when you have an additional display.

## HANDOFF

Thanks to handoff, you can pick up anything right where you left it on another Apple device. Say you're composing an email on your Mac, but you have to leave quickly because you're running late. With Handoff enabled on your iPhone, you may seamlessly continue writing your email there and then.

As long as your devices are still synced with each other over iCloud, Handoff will keep transferring data across your Apple devices for apps like Mail, Safari, Maps, Messages, Reminders, Calendar, Contacts, Pages, Numbers, and Keynote.

Macs running macOS Yosemite or later and iPhones running iOS 8 or later are compatible with this capability. All Apple Watch devices and iPads (4th generation or later) enable handoff.

You may seamlessly transition between Apple devices without losing your position in an application or document thanks to an Apple technology called handoff.

The easiest way to illustrate is with an example.

Let's say you open Mail on your iPad and start replying to an important message. About halfway through, you realize you need to connect a file from your Mac. You may use Handoff to wirelessly move your partly written answer from your iPad to your Mac without having to start over from scratch. Put the file in, then pick up where you left off.

Handoff works with a wide variety of applications, such as:

- Pages
- Numbers
- Keynote
- Mail
- Calendar
- Contacts
- Reminders
- Safari
- Music
- Podcasts

and many third-party apps

When you Handoff to a different device, the app and document you were using remain open in exactly the same state as they were on the first device.

Handoff is the most efficient way to transfer music or podcasts from one Apple device to another. To be more precise, you can even use Handoff, or Universal Clipboard, to copy content from your iPhone and paste it into your Mac.

Handoff allows you to transition between an Apple Watch and other devices, but only between devices like a Mac, iPhone, iPad, iPod touch, or other mobile device.

## HOW TO USE HANDOFF ON AN IPHONE, IPAD, OR MAC

Making use of handoff is simple. Just launch an appropriate app, start using it on the first device, then follow the instructions below to move the app to the second device.

There's nothing more to do with Universal Clipboard if all you want to do with it is copy and paste across different devices. easy material copying and pasting across devices.

## HANDOFF TO AN IPHONE

Swipe up from the bottom of the screen to open the App Switcher (or double-click the Home button if your iPhone has one). Next, click the bottom-of-the-screen banner to see an app icon and the source device's name.

## HANDOFF TO AN IPAD

Use the iPhone method mentioned above to locate an app in the App Switcher view, or go to the Home screen and tap the app icon that appears on the far right side of the Dock. It must be equipped with a little emblem that indicates which machine you are passing over from.

## HANDOFF TO A MAC

Click the program icon that appears in the Dock. Depending on your macOS version, this icon will appear at the far left or far right border of the Dock. It must be equipped with a little emblem that indicates which computer you are handing over control of.

Alternatively, you may launch the App Switcher by pressing Cmd + Tab and choose the app located on the left side. A symbol identifying the device you are handing control to should be included in this app.

## FIX HANDOFF IF IT DOESN'T WORK

Handoff is said to be easier than manually transferring material between two devices. While it seldom breaks, the functionality works well most of the time.

Handoff may not be working as intended for a variety of reasons, but if you follow the tips below, you should be able to fix them.

## SIGN IN TO THE SAME APPLE ID ACCOUNT ON BOTH DEVICES

Make sure the devices you're trying to use Handoff with are both connected into the same Apple ID or iCloud account.

- On an iPhone or iPad, click Settings and choose [Your Name] at the top of the screen to confirm this.
- On a Mac, open System Preferences and choose Apple ID.
- If Handoff is still not functioning, sign out of both devices and then sign back in.

## ENABLE HANDOFF IN THE SETTINGS ON BOTH DEVICES

It's possible that the settings of one or both of the devices you're attempting to use have handoff disabled.

> To enable Handoff on an iPhone or iPad, go to Settings > General >AirPlay& Handoff.
>
> On a linked iPhone, open the Apple Watch app, choose General, then Enable Handoff for an Apple Watch.

Prefer tabs: in full screen ⬍ when opening documents

Ask to keep changes when closing documents

☑ Close windows when quitting an app

When selected, open documents and windows will not be restored when you re-open an app.

Recent items: 10 ⬍ Documents, Apps and Servers

☑ Allow Handoff between this Mac and your iCloud devices

?

On a Mac, choose Allow Handoff between this Mac and your iCloud devices by clicking General in the System Preferences box, and then click OK.

If you are unable to find Handoff in the settings, make sure your device meets the Continuity requirements listed on Apple's website.

## TURN ON WI-FI AND BLUETOOTH

Handoff uses Bluetooth and Wi-Fi to transfer data between your devices. Before verifying that both devices are linked to the same Wi-Fi network, make sure that Bluetooth is enabled in each device's Control Center.

This is also an excellent time to mention that both devices need to be somewhat near to each other (or in the same room) in order for Handoff to work.

## MAKE SURE THE APP IS OPEN ON THE FIRST DEVICE

The most common reason for problems with Handoff is because the app you are trying to transfer isn't active on the first device. All of your current open apps are the only ones that may be transferred; your past use is not taken into account.

This is particularly crucial if you use background-playing music or podcast programs.

Before passing an app across, make sure it's active on the first device you're using. When you open it, try to switch it to another device and use it for a little while.

## CONTINUITY CAMERA

With the introduction of the macOS Ventura update in 2022, Apple improved the Continuity Camera, making it one of the most fascinating Continuity features. While there are many of uses for it, using the iPhone as a Mac's camera and extending FaceTime conversations across Apple devices are the best ones.

Moreover, any photos and documents you scan with your close-by iPhone or iPad will open on your Mac's screen immediately.

Continuity Camera is compatible with almost all native apps that utilize the camera. Macs running macOS Mojave or later and iPhones running iOS 12 or later may both make advantage of this functionality; however, macOS Ventura is required in order to use your iPhone as a camera.

## USING CONTINUITY CAMERA TO REPLACE YOUR MAC'S CAMERA WITH YOUR IPHONE

Before employing Continuity Camera, there are a few things you must be sure of. You need to be running at least macOS Ventura on your Mac and iOS 16 on your iPhone. It is necessary for both devices to be linked to the same wireless network and to have Bluetooth enabled. It operates in a manner similar to that of Apple Device Handoff.

Now that it's over, you may use Continuity Camera.

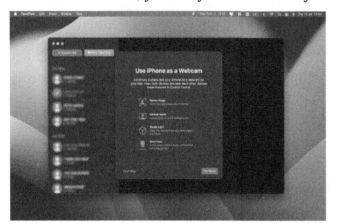

Start your Mac machine and launch FaceTime.

The first time you use FaceTime after updating to Ventura on your macOS system, you'll get a welcome screen explaining how Continuity Camera works.

Navigate to the View tab in the menu bar when the app is open.

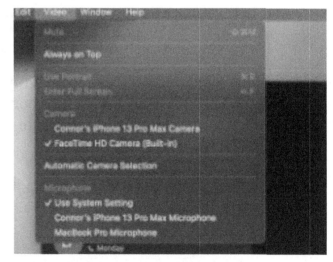

To change the camera on your smartphone, just choose your iPhone from the list.

You will get a notification on your iPhone letting you know that you are connected and occupying the majority of the screen. Additionally, you have the option to pause or disconnect the broadcast.

The webcam for your call will now be the camera on your iPhone.

After your call, you may go back to the View tab and continue using the camera on your Mac. Changes might be made to this at any moment.

If you're using a different app to conduct a video chat, like Zoom, Google Meet, Microsoft Teams, etc. Once there, go to the app's camera options. Select your iPhone there rather than the integrated webcam. The automated procedure will operate in the same way.

## USE VIDEO EFFECTS WITH CONTINUITY CAMERA

When utilizing a camera on a Mac, you may choose from a variety of video effects in the Control Center. Continuity Camera allows you to continue using these effects. There's also a new option called Desk View that uses the ultra-wide lens on the iPhone together with some clever image processing to give you a down-shot of the desk in front of you.

How to activate video effects is as follows:

You may open the Control Center by clicking on the emblem in the menu bar. You may use any keyboard shortcut or hand gestures to do this.

When the Control Center is open, click the Video Effects button at the top.

From here, click on the effect you want to utilize.

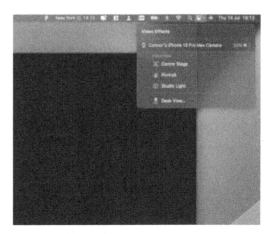

During your video conference, the camera feed will automatically adjust to employ the desired effect.

Most of the video effect options are also available on your Mac's camera, even if Desk View is only enabled while using Continuity Camera.

## APPLE PAY WITH IPHONE OR APPLE WATCH

Apple Pay is a mobile payment and digital wallet service that the company developed. It lets you pay with your Apple devices online, in apps, and in shops.

Using Apple Pay on an iPhone or Apple Watch to make purchases is simple and secure. To use Apple Pay on your Apple smartphone, you must have an Apple Watch 3 or later running watchOS 6 or later. You also need to be using iOS 11 or later on an iPhone 6 or later.

# SYNCHRONIZING YOUR GADGETS AND MAC

Moving and maintaining data between your Mac and your iPhone, iPad, or iPod touch is known as "synching." For example, you may sync your iPhone and Mac together so that, when you upload a movie to your Mac, it appears on your iPhone as well. Books, TV series, podcasts, movies, music, and more may all be synchronized.

The Finder sidebar displays an iPhone, iPad, or iPod touch that is linked to your Mac by USB or USB-C. When you choose the device from the sidebar, options for customizing the software on your device and syncing items with your Mac appear in the Finder window.

Use the button bar at the top of the window to enable synchronization for any kind of media, including music, movies, and TV programs.

Click General in the button bar to get control over the software and data on your device. For example, you may:

- Look for and install the latest current software for your iPhone, iPad, or iPod touch.
- You should back up the data on your smartphone to your Mac or iCloud.
- Handle multiple backups and restore data onto your device from a backup.

## DO I HAVE TO SYNC?

If you own an iPod classic, iPod nano, or iPod shuffle, you need to sync it with your Mac. There is nothing more that can be done to supplement it.

If you own an iPhone, iPad, or iPod touch, you only need to sync with your Mac when you have updated or new content.

Syncing your iPhone, iPad, or iPod Touch is not required. Direct downloads from the iTunes Store, App Store, Apple Books, and other Apple services are available for your devices. You may also use iCloud to keep everything consistent across all of your devices.

## CAN I SELECT TO HAVE ALL OF MY CONTENT AUTOMATICALLY OR JUST PARTICULAR ITEMS SYNCED?

The easiest and fastest way is to have all material automatically sync. To enable synchronization, just tick the "Automatically sync when this [device] is connected" box in the General pane for each kind of material you want to sync. The same content is updated on your iPhone, iPad, and iPod touch each time you connect them to your Mac.

Sync a few things: You may choose to synchronize certain items exclusively. For example, you may choose to sync only a few movies on your iPhone in order to save space. You may still automatically sync everything for other types of content, such as TV shows, podcasts, and books.

## DOES MY IPAD, IPHONES, OR IPOD TOUCH NEED TO BE CONNECTED TO MY MAC IN ORDER TO SYNC?

No. You can sync your devices if your Mac and your iOS-enabled iPhone or iPad are linked to the same wireless network. Before you can establish Wi-Fi syncing, you must first connect your device via a cable, choose it from the sidebar, and then turn on the syncing over Wi-Fi option. See Sync content from your Mac to your iPhone, iPad, or iPod touch via Wi-Fi.

## IF YOU USE ICLOUD, HOW DOES THAT DIFFER FROM SYNCING?

When you use iCloud, moving files between your Mac and iPhone, iPad, or iPod touch is simple and automatic. For example, if you take a picture using iCloud Photos on your iPhone, it will appear on your Mac and other devices soon. When you have iCloud enabled, your Mac, iPhone, iPad, or iPod touch are automatically updated whenever content changes—you don't have to do anything. Visit What Is iCloud? to find out

more.

Use synchronization to arrange the files on your device: By synchronizing, you may securely backup your device's data to your Mac or the iCloud, keep your device up to date with the latest versions of iOS and iPadOS, and, should the need arise, use a backup to restore data from your device.

When you sync, you have complete control over what material is delivered to your device. You may choose which files to sync, or all of them. For example, before a vacation, you may sync a bunch of audiobooks to your iPhone so you can listen to them while driving. By employing synchronization, you may send just the files you need fast.

# CHAPTER ONE
# STAYING CONNECTED

## OPTIONS FOR WIRELESS CONNECTIVITY

### WI-FI

Every Apple MacBook model—including the MacBook Pro and MacBook Air—has built-in wifi adapters. We call them AirPort adapters. Using the AirPort adapter that comes with your MacBook, connect your computer to a Wi-Fi network or access point. From there, any place with a strong enough signal may provide you access to the Internet. Since connecting to the internet is a fundamental need for every computer, Apple positions the AirPort icon for the MacBook on the desktop's top menu bar.

- Select the AirPort icon located in the upper-right corner of the desktop. The AirPort symbol is a collection of circular waves. causing a pull-down menu to appear.

- After that, choose "Turn AirPort on." If this option is not accessible, your MacBook's AirPort adapter is already operational. With the AirPort adaptor switched on, the MacBook occasionally checks for transmissions from adjacent Wi-Fi access points. The pull-down menu contains a list of all entry points that have been found.

- Click the name of an access point to establish a connection. Look under "Tips" if you are unable to locate your access point on the list. If the access point is not secured, the MacBook joins it immediately. If the access point has an encryption key, the MacBook will prompt you to input it.

- Input the access point's encryption key. Click "Join" to establish a connection.

### MAC WON'T CONNECT TO WI-FI?

Connecting your Mac to a Wi-Fi network is typically easy. By choosing the Wi-Fi icon, you may choose the network you wish to join. If required, you can then enter the network password. However, things may not always go as planned in this procedure. I'll teach you how to connect your Mac to a Wi-Fi network even if it won't connect correctly.

## CONFIRM PROPER NETWORK OPERATION

As a first measure towards troubleshooting, confirm that your Wi-Fi network is up and running. The easiest method to do this is to try to connect with other devices.

If another device is able to connect, you will know that your Mac is the problem. But if other devices aren't able to go online, there could be a problem with your Wi-Fi network.

If you're having trouble with your Wi-Fi network, try these fixes:

- First, you want to attempt rebooting the WiFi router. After turning it off and waiting a little while, switch it back on. Usually, this will fix the issue.
- Next, confirm that the connections going to your router are connected properly. If so, it's possible that the cable you're using is broken; try connecting the router with a new one.
- Should none of these methods work, you should attempt getting in touch with your internet service provider (ISP). Perhaps there is a network outage in your region. When you get in touch with your ISP, they may investigate and, if required, dispatch an engineer.

## CHECK RANGE AND INTERFERENCE

When using Wi-Fi, make sure your Mac isn't too far away from the router. Similarly, make sure your router is in the proper location. It should be placed away from obstructions like high walls. Avoid putting it on the edge of your apartment or house; instead, put it in the center.

Verify that your router is not being interfered with by any other means. Keep it away from microwaves, cordless phones, cameras, electrical cables, and other appliances that might emit electrical signals.

Furthermore, some users assert that since Bluetooth signals may interfere with Wi-Fi, turning them off can be advantageous.

## UPDATE MACOS

Checking for software updates is usually a good idea when you encounter system problems. If a newer version of the operating system is available, upgrade it and see if that resolves the problem with your Mac.

To update your computer if you use macOS Ventura, adhere to these instructions:

- From the Apple menu's drop-down menu, choose System Settings.
- Select General in the left pane, then click Software Update on the right.
- Mac is going to search for updates.
- In the event that an update is available, select Update Now.

## FORGET YOUR WI-FI NETWORK

Another step in troubleshooting is to make your Mac forget about the problematic Wi-Fi network.

To do this, open your Mac's network options as shown below:

- Choose System Preferences on your Mac.
- After selecting Wi-Fi in the left pane, click Advanced on the right.
- Scroll down to see the Known Networks list.
- The more icon, shown by three dots within a circle, may be clicked to choose Remove From List.

You will then have to manually re-establish your connection to the WiFi network. Thus, click the Wi-Fi symbol on the right side of the menu bar to choose the preferred network.

## CHECK YOUR TCP/IP SETTINGS

Your Mac's TCP/IP setup controls how it communicates with other devices. It is thus worthwhile to examine them if your Mac is refusing to connect to Wi-Fi. Specifically, you may restore your connection by renewing your lease for the Dynamic Host Configuration Protocol (DHCP). This is due to the fact that it assigns an IP address to your Mac.

These steps will renew it:

- Establish a network connection using Wi-Fi.
- Go to System Preferences, click Network, and then pick Wi-Fi.
- Open Details on the WiFi you are presently connected to, then choose TCP/IP in the resulting box.
- Just choose "Renew DHCP Lease."
- When the question displays, click the blue Apply button.
- Click OK to end the subwindow.

## RUN WIRELESS DIAGNOSTICS

You may inspect and generate a report on your Mac's wireless services using a wireless diagnostics tool that comes with macOS.

To open Wireless Diagnostics, search for it in Spotlight (Cmd + Space). You may work with an IT professional or your internet service provider to solve the problem using the log generated when you follow the on-screen instructions.

## BLUETOOTH

All recent Macs come equipped with Bluetooth, which should allow you to associate a wide range of devices with your computer. It's a simple feature, but certain parts may be difficult to use if you're not acquainted with it. Let us look at how to turn on Bluetooth on a Mac and what steps to do next. Let's examine where to activate Bluetooth on your Mac, how to make sure it works, and the basics of connecting a new device.

## DOES MY MAC HAVE BLUETOOTH?

All modern Mac computers (released in 2011 or after) come with built-in Bluetooth connectivity. There's nothing else you need to buy if you want Bluetooth compatibility on your MacBook Pro, MacBook Air, or iMac.

To use Bluetooth on your Mac, just follow the instructions below to activate it. If you don't see the relevant Bluetooth settings in the System Preferences panel, your Mac most likely doesn't have Bluetooth.

In this case, you may be able to purchase an adaptor to enable Bluetooth on your PC. Since most of them are designed for Windows, make sure the one you choose is marked as compatible with macOS.

You may want to consider purchasing a new Mac if your old one is so old that it isn't compatible with Bluetooth. One of the numerous problems with these old devices is the lack of Bluetooth capability.

## HOW TO TURN ON BLUETOOTH ON MAC

On a Mac, using Bluetooth is easy, but you have to turn it on first. To activate Bluetooth, go to System Preferences from the Apple menu located in the upper-left corner of the screen. Choose Bluetooth from the popup that appears.

On the left side of the Bluetooth panel are the Bluetooth icon and its current state. To enable Bluetooth, click the Turn Bluetooth On button if it's not already enabled.

That's all it takes to turn on Bluetooth on a Mac. While you're here, I recommend checking the Show Bluetooth in menu bar box if it's not already turned on. By doing this, you'll be able to access Bluetooth connections without always coming back to this panel since a Bluetooth icon will show up at the top of your screen.

## HOW TO CONNECT BLUETOOTH DEVICES TO YOUR MAC

With Bluetooth switched on, let's see how to connect gadgets to your Mac. Before using a Bluetooth device on your Mac for the first time, you have to link it with it. If you've used Bluetooth on other devices in the past, you should be acquainted with the idea of discoverability.

Since several Bluetooth devices are usually adjacent to one another, you have to manually couple devices for security reasons. You can only do this while the device is discoverable, commonly known as "pairing mode". As indicated before, your Mac's Bluetooth settings window must be open in order for your PC to be discovered.

## PAIRING NEW BLUETOOTH DEVICES TO YOUR MAC

In macOS, the Bluetooth pairing process varies based on the device you want to link. Most other operating systems, including Windows, Android, and iOS, set themselves as discoverable when you have the Bluetooth preferences page open. The exact process to switch on pairing mode differs from device to device for those without a graphical user interface, such Bluetooth mice, keyboards, headphones, and other similar products.

This usually means holding down the Power button for a few seconds or hitting many buttons at once. See your device's user manual for further information. When the second device is prepared for pairing, its name ought to appear under Devices in the Bluetooth settings on your Mac. Click the Connect button next to the person you wish to add.

For many Bluetooth devices, you have to make sure the PIN entered on both devices match. Verify this, especially if you're in a busy area with lots of electronics. If you have to manually enter a PIN (typically for older devices only), stick to a conventional sequence such as 0000, 1111, or 1234.

This completes the pairing process between your Mac and the other device via Bluetooth. Once both are switched on and within around 30 feet of one other, they will automatically connect. This eliminates the need for you to repeat the pairing process every time you want to utilize the same device.

You can always manually connect your gadgets if they don't connect automatically. The Bluetooth settings panel's Devices section lists all of your previously associated devices, along with a menu bar icon shortcut for each. Make sure the device is powered on before double-clicking its name to establish a connection. Disconnect the linked device from any other paired PCs first if this does not work. When used with numerous devices at once, most Bluetooth devices will have problems, while the most recent Bluetooth standards are striving to remedy this.

Choose Remove with a right-click to remove a device from the list. The device will no longer connect automatically once you do this; you will have to pair it again in order to use it.

## UNDERSTANDING THE MACOS BLUETOOTH ICON

If you've activated the Bluetooth menu bar icon, as previously suggested, you'll always see the Bluetooth logo there. It allows you to rapidly view the complete options panel, connect to a device, and switch on or off Bluetooth.

The Bluetooth status will determine the icon's modification. When Bluetooth is switched on, it displays a straightforward icon. In the meanwhile, the Bluetooth logo will have a slash across it if Bluetooth is switched off. Other graphic modifications were made to the Bluetooth icon in earlier versions of macOS to transmit relevant information. Unfortunately, Apple eliminated them with the release of macOS Big Sur.

Whenever there's a minimum of one Bluetooth device linked to your Mac, you'll see the Bluetooth symbol with three dots above it on previous versions of macOS. When there is a Bluetooth problem, you may also notice a zigzag line above the symbol. If you notice this, restart your Mac, and then go through Bluetooth troubleshooting.

## TURNING ON BLUETOOTH ON YOUR MAC WITHOUT A MOUSE OR KEYBOARD

Many individuals use a Bluetooth mouse and/or keyboard with their desktop Mac. As one would anticipate, because you need those devices to access the Bluetooth menu, having Bluetooth abruptly switched off might create problems here.

Thankfully, until a USB mouse is attached, macOS does not turn off Bluetooth on Macs without a trackpad. If your Mac isn't detecting a mouse or keyboard, the Bluetooth Setup Assistant ought to appear. Nevertheless, you may use only a mouse or keyboard to re-enable Bluetooth on your Mac in case anything goes wrong with those tools.

A MacBook's built-in trackpad and keyboard eliminate this problem. To do this on an iMac, however, you'll need to attach a USB mouse or keyboard. Use the keyboard shortcut Cmd + Space to launch Spotlight search and activate Bluetooth without a mouse. Look for Bluetooth File Exchange and hit Return to open it. A prompt stating that Bluetooth is disabled will show when you run the application.

Go back and accept the Bluetooth activation popup. Open Spotlight once again, enter System Preferences, and use the menu's search box to find Bluetooth if you need to visit the Bluetooth panel. Use your mouse to browse to the System Preferences panel or the Bluetooth menu bar icon if a keyboard is not available.

## AIRDROP

There has been a lot written about AirDrop since its launch in 2011. Almost ten years ago, AirDrop was a wonderful addition to the Apple ecosystem. It lingered and suffered, finally slipping behind a number of other services.

Although correct at the time, the critique is now untrue. In recent years, Apple has improved the speed at which AirDrop loads and the accuracy with which it detects devices. I'll walk you through setting up AirDrop on your Mac and other devices, as well as several easy-to-use programs for file transfers.

### HOW DOES AIRDROP WORK?

AirDrop's objective is simple: to transmit files. It recognizes adjacent devices that are compatible with Bluetooth and WiFi for file transfers. Files from anybody or only the people on your contact list may be accepted. You may also tell AirDrop to stop accepting any file transfers at all, but this would make your device inaccessible to other people and will stop you from transferring anything.

With OS X Yosemite, AirDrop on the Mac entered a new era. Earlier versions of OS X (now macOS) did not support AirDrop for Mac and iOS. This made file transfers between a Mac and an iPhone or iPad challenging; however, this is no longer a problem since these devices now function flawlessly together.

On the Mac and iPhone, where is AirDrop located? Users often ask this question, but because AirDrop isn't a stand-alone software, it's difficult to respond to. Simply choose AirDrop from the share-sheet when you right-click on a file or folder, then choose AirDrop to share the file. There will be a list of devices that are accessible for sharing.

## HOW TO TURN ON AIRDROP ON MAC

Though it may not function on all devices, Apple goods come with AirDrop. Let's see how to make AirDrop available on Mac. Even though AirDrop is a highly easy and efficient way to share files, Apple does not make it easily accessible on the Mac. Here's how to make AirDrop available on a Mac:

- Launch the Mac's Finder application.
- From the Favorites area on the window's left side, choose "AirDrop".
- Choose your preferred discoverability option from the list of options at the bottom of the window when you run AirDrop on Mac.

Note: Any Apple device nearby will be able to send you files if you choose "Everyone" from this list. Remember this the next time you're in public.

Because it lets anybody upload files to your Mac, iPhone, or iPad, AirDrop may pose a security concern. Malware may inadvertently get onto your device if you click on a link or file that contains it!

## MANUAL FOR IPHONE TO MAC AIRDROP

The easiest method to airdrop from Mac to iPhone is via the Dropzone software. Just start dragging a picture or group of photos. You'll see the Dropzone symbol emerge. Your iPhone will receive the image(s) you drop onto the Dropzone AirDrop icon.

Another way to distribute files from a Mac to iPhones or iPads is to right-click. This is how it's done:

- Find the file that needs to be sent to an iPhone.
- Go to the "AirDrop" sub-menu and pick it.
- Perform a right-click on the image or filename.
- Go to "Share" by scrolling down from the drop-down menu.
- Choose the device to which you want to transfer a file or folder from the new window that opens.

## AIRDROP A WORD, EXCEL, OR POWERPOINT FILE

You may wish to AirDrop your file straight from Word, Excel, or PowerPoint while working on it to avoid wasting time looking for it in Finder. It is simple:

- Find the Share button in Word, Excel, or PowerPoint, then click it.
- Sharing choices will be shown to you. Choosing "Send a Copy"
- Click the sharing symbol to open a new window and choose AirDrop.

- When a popup displaying nearby devices shows up, choose the one you wish to AirDrop your file to.

## HOW TO AIRDROP FROM IPHONE TO MAC

Let's now examine the process of AirDropping to a laptop. On iOS and iPadOS, there are several differences when sending files over AirDrop. Here's how you do it:

- Choose the picture, document, website, or other content you want to share.
- Click the "share sheet" icon, which is a box with an arrow pointing upward, at the bottom of the screen.
- Click on "AirDrop" in the menu. Note: Your device may show up in the top row if the device you want to transfer the file to has AirDrop enabled and your device may transmit files to it as a contact.
- Select the Mac that you want to send the file to.

## WHY AIRDROP IS NOT WORKING ON MY MAC

There are a few things to check while utilizing AirDrop on your Mac, particularly if you're experiencing problems. Here are some things to consider:

Your Mac is old. Does earlier Mac OS X support AirDrop? Sure, but not to the same extent as more modern Macs. If you are using an earlier version of macOS than Yosemite or have an older Mac that does not support AirDrop, this may be a problem. It's possible that the AirDrop protocol is incompatible with your devices if your Mac is older.

Your Mac's settings are turned off. Remember that you have three choices when using AirDrop: accept files from contacts, accept files from everyone, or refuse to accept any AirDrop files at all. As I said before, if your AirDrop settings are set to "No One," you are unable to transmit or receive files.

The settings on your iPad or iPhone are off. Similar to Macs, iPhones and iPads provide three AirDrop choices. Check the AirDrop settings on any of these devices if you are unable to transmit or receive from any of them.

The gadget cannot be used as a contact. If you have AirDrop set to "Contacts Only," then only files from contacts will be accepted. It's conceivable that none of the accounts linked to any of your contacts are being used by your device. If your work phone was using your work email as its account but that email was not shown in your contacts card in Settings, your Mac would not identify the contact. New gadgets may also have this problem.

WiFi and Bluetooth don't work correctly. Files may be sent and received via Bluetooth or WiFi using AirDrop. Unless it's public WiFi or anything is stopping your devices from connecting, you should not have any issues if you are on the same WiFi network (a VPN, for example). Putting both devices' Bluetooth on is also a smart idea.

# FACETIME, IMESSAGE, AND OTHER COMMUNICATION TOOLS

If, like me, you would like to write on your laptop's keyboard rather than the small iPhone keypad, or if you just don't want to switch devices to answer a text or call, you can set up your Mac to accept calls and texts from your iPhone. With an Apple ID, you can send messages and make calls online using the Messages and FaceTime applications on your Mac.

To send SMS messages via your carrier instead of the internet or make calls using cellular service, your Mac must be running OS X Yosemite or later, and your iPhone must be running iOS 8.1 or later.

Note: If you follow these steps, your contacts won't be synced between your Mac and iPhone. To do that, you'll need to sync them or set up iCloud contacts.

## SIGN IN TO IMESSAGES WITH YOUR APPLE ID

Initially, make sure that the Apple ID you are using to login into Messages on your Mac and iPhone is the same. Here's how it works:

Go to on your iPhone to check your Apple ID. "Settings" > "Messages" > "Send & Receive"

Open the Messages app on your Mac to check your Apple ID. Select "Preferences" from the drop-down menu after clicking "Messages" in the menu bar. Select "iMessage" from the window's top menu.

## SET UP TEXT MESSAGE FORWARDING

To configure your Mac to receive SMS messages from your phone:

- Then choose "Text Message Forwarding."
- Go to Settings on your iPhone.
- Scroll down to the "Messages" section.
- Turn on the switch that is next to the name of your laptop.

## SET UP FACETIME AND ICLOUD

Make that your iPhone and Mac are linked to the same Wi-Fi network and are logged into FaceTime and iCloud with the same Apple ID. Here's how it works:

Using your iPhone, choose "Settings." You should be able to see your Apple ID at the top of the settings window. You may scroll down and choose "FaceTime" to see which account is currently active.

Click the Apple symbol located in the top-left corner of your Mac's screen, then choose "System Preferences." Make sure you are signed into the right Apple account. Launch the FaceTime application, choose "FaceTime" from the upper menu bar's drop-down menu, and then choose "Preferences" from the drop-down menu. At the top of the window, you can see the account you are now logged into.

## ALLOW CALLS ON OTHER DEVICES

On your iPhone, you must now turn on a few settings:

After navigating to Settings on your iPhone, tap "Phone".

Use "Calls on Other Devices."

Turning on "Allow Calls on Other Devices" is necessary.

Make sure you are in "Calls on Other Devices" when your Mac is still powered on.

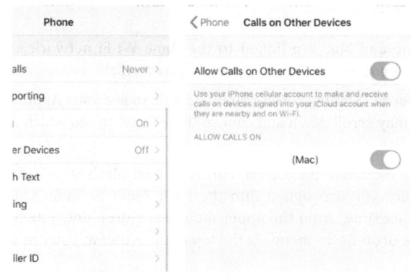

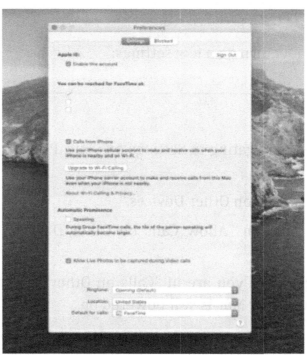

On your Mac, open the FaceTime application.

Upon selecting "FaceTime" from the menu bar at the top of the screen, a drop-down menu titled "Preferences" will appear.

Select "Settings" from the menu that appears.

Make sure that the "Calls from iPhone" option is checked.

Keep in mind that in order for you to receive calls on your phone, your devices need to be near each other and linked to the same Wi-Fi network. To answer calls when your Mac is linked to a separate Wi-Fi network, use Wi-Fi calling.

## SET UP WI-FI CALLING

If Wi-Fi Calling is supported by your Mac, phone (iPhone 5S or later), and carrier, you may use it to make calls via the internet instead of using cellular connection. You can also make calls from devices that are not connected to the same Wi-Fi networks as your phone and while your phone is off, depending on your carrier.

- • On your iPhone, choose "Wi-Fi Calling" from "Settings" > "Phone".
- Turn on the feature "Wi-Fi Calling on This iPhone." A pop-up window will advise you of how it provides your carrier with location data. Click "Enable."

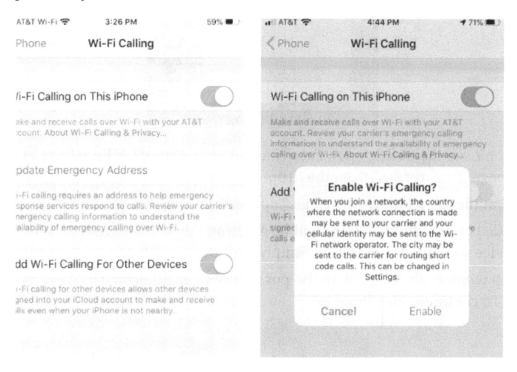

- Toggle "Add Wi-Fi Calling For Other Devices." When you utilize Wi-Fi calling to dial 911, your carrier may route the call to an emergency response center based on your stored emergency address or automatically gathered geographical data. You could get a notification from your carrier about 911 calls, invoicing, and Wi-Fi calling that contains this information. Click "Continue" at the bottom of the notification.
- When making emergency calls, you have to provide an address if location data is not available. You may update your address if your carrier has already recorded it for you (such as your billing address). To do so, click the blue "Update Emergency Address" button in the middle of the page, then follow the on-screen instructions.

## YOU MUST NOW SET UP YOUR MAC.

You may see a notice appear on your Mac after turning on Wi-Fi calling on your phone. Depending on your scenario, when you click "Turn On," you'll either be sent to the main FaceTime menu or the Preferences window. You will be informed, via a tiny display, that emergency callers will be able to locate you. Click "OK" to confirm that you agree.

- If you don't see the notice, open FaceTime on your Mac, click FaceTime in the menu bar, then choose "Preferences" from the drop-down menu.

- Verify that the top window's "Settings" option is chosen.

- Under "Calls from iPhone," there will be a button labeled "Upgrade to Wi-Fi Calling" once your device supports Wi-Fi calling. Simply click it.

- A pop-up window alerting you to the possibility of location sharing with your carrier will appear. To continue, click "Enable".

An emergency contact address is also needed here. After you choose "Update to Wi-Fi Calling," this button will be replaced with one that says "Update Emergency Address." Click that to see and, if required, change your address.

You're done now!

# STAYING PRODUCTIVE WITH MACOS PRODUCTIVITY FEATURES, MANAGING FILES AND ORGANIZING YOUR DATA EFFECTIVELY

One of the many attractive features of Macs is its easy-to-use interface and simplistic design. But, a mac user may get insane if their computer starts to fill up with data and becoming messy.

This might make your Mac sluggish and make finding the required file difficult. Let's discuss some top tips for Mac file management so you can increase productivity and maintain a clutter-free virtual workspace!

## NAMING AND VIEWING YOUR FILES

Let's start from the ground up. By the exact method you use to store files on your Mac, that is. Establishing an effective file system is essential to swiftly identifying and gaining access to them. So, giving your folders more specific names is our first tip for organizing files on a Mac. Provide file names with data such as versions, dates, and project names to facilitate future file searches. You may even provide a short explanation.

Remember all the other ways that Finder allows you to see your files as well:

Use the Finder's Sort By function to arrange files according to name, file size, updated date, and other parameters.

- Use the search function in Finder to look for certain file types and be sure to include file extensions in your query. For example, to locate a Keynote presentation, put ".key" into the search field.

- To see a preview of the file without opening it, use the spacebar while it is chosen.

By following these tips, you may locate and organize files with ease.

## SAVING YOUR FILES

I also suggest using "Save as" instead than "Save" more often. In the end, this will save time even if it will require a few more clicks. Selecting "Save as" removes the need to transfer files from your documents or downloads folder to more suitable directories where they belong all along. To enter the store As box, just press Command + Shift + S. From there, you can name your file and choose where to store it.

## MAC FOLDER STRUCTURE BEST PRACTICES

Although most people know how to create folders, are you really utilizing them to manage your files? When you have all many files, it might be tempting to just put them all in one folder. However, this will just lead to further problems down the road. I suggest using the following recommended practices for organizing files on a Mac:

### GROUP BY FILE TYPE

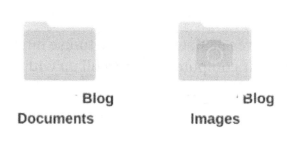

Blog Documents    Blog Images

Create separate folders for your images, movies, music, and documents. You will be able to locate the required files more quickly and easily as a result, since you will be aware of the precise location of each kind of file.

### USE FOLDERS FOR DIFFERENT PROJECTS

If you work on many projects at once, you should be very precise about each folder's purpose. You may wish to create a folder and add the required files to it for each project. Make distinct folders for files pertaining to your professional and personal tasks. To prevent mixing up various files and notions, you may keep your concentration by arranging your files according to medium and purpose.

### RELOCATE BACKUPS AND OLD VERSIONS

To "declutter" your primary folders rapidly, think about creating a separate folder for backups and older versions of data. You may locate the most current versions of your files and make space available by doing this. When you're certain you no longer need these backups, you may easily remove the whole folder. more space for storing.

### USE IMAGES AS FOLDER ICONS

While designating photos as folder icons can seem a little excessive, productivity can really be increased by doing so. We process pictures faster than words, so using an image as a folder icon may make it quicker for you to locate the folder you're searching for. This is particularly helpful if you have a number of folders with identical names. To designate a picture as a folder icon, follow these steps:

Choose the desired picture file on your Mac, then copy its contents to the Clipboard. Make sure the image is clear and high resolution before utilizing it as a folder icon. To add the picture, control-click the folder in Finder, then choose Get Info from the shortcut menu. Click the little folder symbol at the top of the informative pane in the Get Info box.

After pasting the picture, hit Command-V. To get the same result, drag an image file into the folder icon. The picture will now be the folder's icon. To get the original folder icon back, just click the folder icon and then Command + X.

## MAC FILE ORGANIZATION USING SMART FOLDERS

Smart Folders are one of the most inventive and undervalued Mac features. You're missing out if you haven't started utilizing them yet. Smart Folders are essentially stored searches that look like ordinary folders. This suggests that you won't need to go through all of Finder's locations in order to swiftly retrieve every file related to your search.

This is how to arrange files on a Mac using Smart Folders:

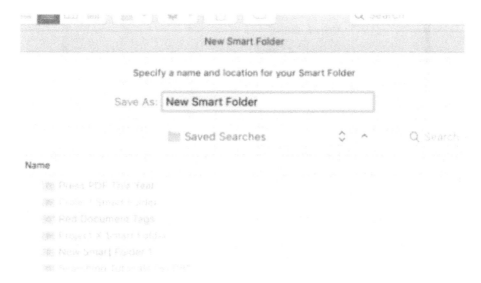

- To launch a new Finder window, press Command + Option, or choose File > New Smart Folder from the menu.

- The search box that appears may be used to define the criteria for your smart folder.

- Type in parameters such as subject, search term, date, etc., and choose from the produced choices that show up below the search.

- You may expand your search parameters by clicking the "+" icon next to the Save option.

- When you're done, click Save and choose the location and name of your Smart folder.

The nicest thing about Smart Folders is that they don't really relocate your stuff. They just generate a reference to all of the relevant files so that you can easily find them later.

# HOW TO ORGANIZE FILES ON MAC DESKTOP

A chaotic desktop is inconvenient because it takes up RAM, which slows down your Mac's performance, and makes things hard to discover.

You should thus keep your data online in the best possible order.

## DECLUTTERING FILES ON YOUR DESKTOP

Using the view settings on your Mac, sort them out to make some desktop space.

To begin creating your desktop from scratch, remove every icon off your screen. Next, follow these steps to utilize Finder to choose certain files to display:

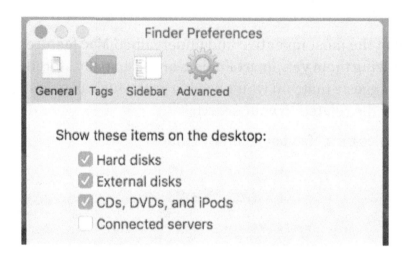

- •Click the Finder icon to bring up a menu, then choose Finder Preferences.
- Click the General tab and choose the file types you wish to see on your desktop.
- For example, you may wish to check the box next to "Show these items on the desktop" for external drives if you often interact with photos and films taken from SD cards.

Assume for a moment that you would want to organize the things that are on your desktop. You can more easily notice the things that are worth saving by selecting the Sort By option. To sort the files by name, size, or date created or edited, just choose the Sort By option from the View menu on your desktop.

After decluttering, you may choose how to organize the remaining files by using the Clean Up By option.

## USING STACKS

If you're experiencing problems making your desktop icons smaller, consider placing them in Stacks. This macOS feature lets you organize your files into neat little groupings. You may either click View on your desktop and choose Use Stacks, or you can just drag and drop files on top of each other to form a stack. After that, you may arrange them according to the dates on which they were added, changed, etc.

## DESKTOP MINIMALISM

Going ahead, make every effort to organize your desktop in a simple way. Think of it this way: Only use your desktop for tasks that really need your quick attention. To ensure rapid access, only create shortcuts to the programs and folders you use often.

## MAC FILE ORGANIZATION USING MAC TAGS

One of the most overlooked aspects of Mac is tags. With this functionality, users may label files for easy and rapid access in the future. You may use tags to organize different files and media pieces without having to move them. #Really cool.

This is an explanation on how to tag your files:

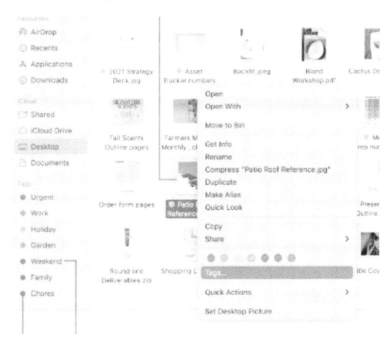

- • When you right-click a file, a shortcut menu will display. Choose Tags.
- •Enter a new tag name or choose from the list of already-existing tags in the window that pops up.
- • In order to add additional tags to the file, press Return after each tag name.
- Select distinct hues for every tag.

Once files are tagged, you may manage them using the Finder's left sidebar.

Here are some creative ideas for tags:

For workflows:

Active | Archive | Completed

For general/personal matters:

Urgent |To-do | Bills | References | To delete, etc.

## FILES SYNCING WITH ICLOUD DRIVE

Finally, if you use many devices and are often on the road, iCloud Drive can help you access and update important data. You can even preserve the same organizational structure you put so much effort into creating while synchronizing files!

This is the operation of iCloud Drive:

iCloud Drive is installed automatically on every current Apple device running the most recent operating system..

- Mac users may activate iCloud Drive by heading to System Preferences, selecting iCloud, and then selecting iCloud Drive.
- Although you have the option to choose which files and folders to sync, your Desktop and Documents folders will automatically be saved to iCloud.
- Any modifications made to those documents will be automatically synced to all of your devices that have iCloud Drive enabled.
- iCloud Drive will save your freshly produced documents in addition to the places you choose.
- You may also see the files in your iCloud Drive by entering into your iCloud account on iCloud.com. This suggests that a Windows-based computer may be used to view these files.

# CHAPTER TWO

# MASTERING MAC SECURITY AND PRIVACY

Although Macs are less likely to be targeted since there are fewer Macs than PCs—in fact, the amount of malware on Macs is declining—Mac users may be a highly profitable target and are thus considered worth the effort. Thus, Macs might be the target of malware and viruses.

Even Craig Federighi, Apple's director of software, said during the company's trial against Epic that "we have a level of malware on the Mac that we don't find acceptable." He meant to emphasize the benefits of restricting owners of iPhones and iPads to exclusively download software from the iOS App Store, but what's important to remember is that even Apple employees are aware that Mac infections exist.

On the other hand, Macs are often safer than PCs. This is partially because Apple maintains such strict control over the hardware and software, and the Mac operating system is Unix-based, making it more difficult to abuse. Furthermore, Macs are safer because of the many security mechanisms and safeguards built into the Mac and Mac OS X, which make them more difficult to compromise.

That does not, however, mean that you should consider your Mac to be unbreakable. Apple has to take the security mechanisms included into macOS seriously in order to safeguard its consumers, since viruses and hackers have been targeting Macs.

Remember that the M-series chips, which Apple started using in November 2020, are more secure than Intel CPUs. However, Silver Sparrow malware was found on the M1 Mac shortly after it was introduced.

## HOW APPLE PROTECTS YOUR MAC

Apple offers many methods to safeguard your Mac from malware and viruses, as you will discover subsequently. Of course, you may take further measures to reinforce these safety measures, such as encrypting your connection using a VPN or installing antivirus software. It's also crucial to exercise caution and avoid clicking on questionable websites or reading mysterious emails. But can you be certain that your parents wouldn't act in the same manner? Thankfully, a Mac has built-in security features that ought to keep even non-techies secure. Here is a list of them.

## SOFTWARE AND SECURITY UPDATES

Because Apple ensures that security updates are often sent out to Macs, keep your Mac software up to date. Apple takes the hassle out of updating your Mac automatically; you don't even have to do this. Follow these instructions to set up your Mac to automatically update software and look for updates:

- • Go to System Preferences (the version of System Settings before Ventura).
- • Next, click Software Update in the General section.
- • Verify whether Automatic Updates are enabled. This ought to guarantee that your Mac downloads the most recent software from Apple.

While certain security updates may be delivered to your Mac and installed as background updates without needing a restart, regular software updates still need to be restarted.

To guarantee that you get background updates as soon as Apple publishes them, make sure that Install Security Responses and System Files—or "Install system data files and security updates" on prior OSs—is chosen in Ventura.

Under System Settings > General > Software Update in Ventura, you may find this. Next to Automatic Updates, choose the (i).

Before Ventura, this was located in System Preferences > Software Update > Advanced.

By accelerating the release of security updates for the Mac, iPhone, and iPad, Rapid Security Responses go one step further in this regard. The capability will be available in iOS 16.3 and macOS Ventura 13.2 from Apple.

Upon restarting your Mac, any Rapid Security Responses will take effect instantly. Apple is able to provide security patches more swiftly and separately from bigger upgrades by using this technique.

## APP PROTECTIONS

Keep your program selection limited to Mac program Store titles if you want total assurance while installing any software. You can be sure that no software in the Mac software Store will put you at danger since Apple has vetted every one of them. Apple even goes one step further and mandates that applications disclose to you how they use your data, so you can be sure that no personal information is disclosed to third parties without your consent.

But even programs that aren't downloaded from the Mac App Store will be examined by Apple before being installed; this is what Gatekeeper is for, as I previously said. Gatekeeper checks the file for viruses and harmful code and confirms that the developer has received Apple's verification. Sometimes you may wish to launch a Mac program that was developed by an unidentified developer; in this situation, use care.

The requirement that all programs sold via the Mac App Store support sandboxing is another reason to choose App Store apps over other apps. Apps' access to a Mac's data and resources is restricted by the sandbox.

Ever since macOS 10.15 Catalina was released in 2019, Apple has required all Mac programs to be notarized before they can be started. Furthermore, regardless of where your files are stored—on your Mac, in iCloud Drive, or on external volumes—all Mac programs now need your permission to access them. MacOS will also prompt you to provide permission before an app can use the camera or microphone or record your keystrokes.

## SAFE SURFING

While the aforementioned is meant to shield you against dangerous programs, phishing emails, websites, and online services pose a greater risk. Apple's web browser, Safari, offers a number of additional capabilities related to online security. When you visit a dubious website, Safari will alert you and stop you from visiting it. Since each web page loads as a distinct process in a different tab, you may shut that tab without causing Safari to crash.

Apple also keeps Flash off Macs to safeguard Mac users. One of the most popular ways malware enters computers is via Flash. In 2010, Apple stopped including Flash preinstalled with Safari. Consequently, users had to install Flash themselves in order to add it, so they had to get used to life without it. Early in 2020, Apple discontinued supporting Flash, and as of December 31, 2020, Adobe, the company that created Flash, has also ceased supporting it. Moreover, JavaScript creates certain security vulnerabilities. It's simple to deactivate JavaScript in Safari.

- To disable JavaScript, just go to Safari > Preferences > Security > and uncheck the box next to it. It should be noted that doing this may cause certain online graphics to cease appearing; in the event that this happens, reapply it.

Apple safeguards your privacy in addition to your online security. For instance, Apple uses Intelligent Tracking Prevention to stop online advertising from following users. Customers may see a Privacy Report that details every cross-site tracker that Apple has disabled so that it cannot profile them.

## LOCKDOWN MODE

In the event that you fall prey to a cyberattack, you may use this additional protection feature in macOS Ventura. To stop the assault from taking advantage of you, you may utilize it to fortify your Mac's defenses and impose stringent limitations.

- • Select Lockdown Mode from the System Settings > Privacy & Security menu, click Turn On next to the Lockdown Mode name, input your administrator password, and select Turn On & Restart to activate it.

You may exit Lockdown Mode and resume whenever you think the danger has subsided.

## PASSWORD PROTECTIONS

Additionally, Apple keeps track of your passwords and offers assistance in changing them to more secure ones, suggests strong passwords, and even notifies you in the event that it believes your password may have been compromised in a data breach. Having said that, Apple also offers iCloud Keychain, a password management tool that syncs with all of your Apple gadgets and lets you access apps and services on any of them without having to remember unique login credentials. This has the benefit of allowing you to utilize strong passwords in place of easily remembered ones (which Apple can create for you). Your master password, which is secured with two factor authentication (2FA) for further protection, conceals all of your passwords.

Another method Apple tries to safeguard you is with passkeys, which with macOS Ventura and iOS 16 replace passwords as a simpler and safer way to sign in. Passkeys are safer since everything is end-to-end encrypted and there isn't a password that might be stolen. A distinct passkey is generated for each website or service, which is then stored on your device and in your iCloud Keychain to enable cross-device access. All you have to do is use your Touch ID or Face ID to authenticate. This is new, so it hasn't been extensively utilized yet, but it should make things safer in the future.

## ICLOUD PRIVATE RELAY (ALMOST A VPN)

iCloud Private Relay is only available to those with an iCloud+ membership, but it may help you protect your privacy while using Safari to explore the web. iOS 15 included it. Your whole Safari surfing is encrypted and routed via Apple's proxy server when you use Private Relay, keeping your ISP from seeing what you are doing online.

It's not exactly like a VPN, but it's close. There are many reasons why using a VPN is recommended. One big advantage of utilizing a VPN, which is being able to hide the location of your connection, is not possible with Apple's approach, which is restricted to Safari.

- Click on the slider to turn it on.
- Open System Settings
- Click Firewall
- Click Network
- If you want to specify additional security settings click on Options.

## POST VENTURA

- Choose the Firewall tab in the System Preferences > Security & Privacy pane.
- Click the padlock symbol in the lower left corner to access system settings (you'll be required for your login password).

## CLICK THE TURN ON FIREWALL BUTTON.

Click the Firewall Options button, then choose the Enable Stealth Mode box that pops up. When you complete this step, your computer will be almost undetectable on public networks, such as the free Wi-Fi at coffee shops.

- From the Firewall tab, choose Firewall Options to make changes. Here is a list of applications and services that are able to receive incoming connections.
- For example, if an error notice appears when you attempt to launch an app telling you that it cannot accept an incoming connection, click the "+" next to the list.

It's crucial to keep in mind that while helpful, macOS's Firewall offers only average protection against viruses. This is due to the fact that it only shields you from inbound traffic. It is in charge of limiting which applications and services are allowed to accept incoming connections. It provides no control over connections created by applications and services or connections that go outward. As a result, if you download malware, the macOS firewall won't stop it from connecting to the internet.

Some also choose to limit outbound network connections, so that specific programs cannot "phone home" without their awareness. Additionally, this implies that malware that was inadvertently installed cannot stealthily leak your data.

## FILEVAULT

Apple offers FileVault as a tool to encrypt your data and safeguard it in the event that your Mac is stolen or compromised. If your Mac includes an M-series processor, this encryption goes one step further and protects your login details using specific hardware.

If you are using Ventura, go to System Preferences > Security & Privacy; if you are using an older version of Windows, go to System Settings > Privacy & Security.

Just remember that in order to access your data, you'll need to enter your login password or recovery key, so chances are high you'll lose it if you don't have one of these.

## FIND MY & ACTIVATION LOCK

In the event that your Mac is stolen, Apple also provides extra tools like Find My, which allows you to monitor and maybe even locate your lost computer while also wiping it clean to prevent your data from falling into the wrong hands. Macs with the T2 chip and M1 Macs also come with the Activation Lock feature of Find My, which lets you remotely lock your Mac so that only you can use it.

Some Macs come equipped with Touch ID, a fingerprint scanner that serves as an additional security safeguard. It works for Mac unlocking, software and service logins, and Apple Pay. Therefore, Apple will safeguard your Mac in the event that it is stolen or used maliciously by someone. Apple also provides security against abuse, control over data accessibility, and prevention against harmful applications. If your Mac contains an M-series chip or the T2 security chip—which is included in certain Intel Macs—you may use Activation Lock to ensure that only you will be able to wipe and reactivate it in the event that it is lost or stolen.

# CHAPTER THREE

# TROUBLESHOOTING AND MAINTENANCE

In general, using a Mac is a hassle-free experience. Daily issues are quite uncommon, and many customers have been using their systems without any issues for years. However, because to their complexity, Macs are susceptible to issues that impair performance, such as viruses, applications that behave strangely, and network issues.

Think of your Mac like a vehicle. A automobile may continue to function well for years if maintenance is neglected, but eventually the car will catch up with you and break down in the middle of nowhere. A car's lifetime is increased by years with regular maintenance that maintains it in good condition. This same holds true for your Mac. It will look after you if you look after it.

## TROUBLESHOOTING YOUR MAC

Acting up refers to the possibility of certain programs crashing or macOS being slow or unresponsive. Most of those issues may be easily resolved by following the procedures given below. These are the procedures that Apple support will likely want you to follow when you phone or tweet them.

### FIX COMMON MAC PROBLEMS

Please note that not all issues need you to follow those procedures, especially stages 8 through 10.

- Create a new user account
- Reboot Mac
- Delete Caches folders
- Reset PRAM/NVRAM
- Boot into Safe Mode
- Repair disk permissions

- Reinstall macOS
- Verify disk (and repair if necessary)
- Reset SMC
- Reset Safari and clear caches
- Update to the latest version of macOS

## 1. REBOOT MAC

Depending on the nature of the issue, restarting your computer can be the simplest fix. This is particularly valid in cases when a particular program is behaving strangely. I suggest quickly restarting a Mac as the first course of action.

## 2. RESET PRAM AND NVRAM

How do NVRAM and PRAM function? via apple.com

Even while your Mac is off, it retains some settings in a dedicated memory space (unless there's a battery issue, which we'll cover later). On Macs with Intel processors, this is stored in NVRAM memory; on Macs with PowerPC processors, it is stored in PRAM memory.

Reset PRAM and NVRAM by following these steps:

- Turn off the computer.
- Turn the computer on.
- Press and hold the Command, Option, P, and R keys until you hear the starting sound.
- Until the computer restarts and the starting sound plays twice, keep hitting the keys.
- Let go of the keys.

## 3. BOOT INTO SAFE MODE

To enter Safe Mode when your Mac resumes, press and hold the shift key until a progress bar appears at the bottom of the screen. This indicates that your Mac is booting up in Safe Mode, which removes a few unnecessary caches. After going into Safe Mode, restart normally without using the Shift key.

## 4. RESET THE SYSTEM MANAGEMENT CONTROLLER (SMC)

Resetting the SMC requires various actions depending on whether you're using a MacBook or a desktop computer (such an iMac or Mac Mini). The following is a list of the steps for both platforms:

## HOW TO RESET A DESKTOP'S SMC

- Turn off your MacBook.
- Take out the power cord.
- Give it 15 seconds to pause.
- Reattach the power supply.
- Press and hold the power button on your Mac for five seconds to turn it on.
- How to Reset the SMC Non-Removable Battery on a MacBook
- Switch off your MacBook.
- Take off the USB-C or MagSafe power adapter from the MacBook.
- Press the power button and Shift-Control-Option on the left side of the built-in keyboard at the same time. For ten seconds, hold down both the power button and these keys.* Switch off each key.
- Put the power cable back on.
- You may hit the power button again to restart your Mac.

## 5. REPAIR DISK PERMISSIONS

Fixing disk permissions is no longer necessary since OS X El Capitan preserves file system permissions automatically. If you are still on OS X Yosemite or a previous version, please continue reading. You should periodically fix the disk permissions even if your Mac is running well.

To do this, pick your primary hard drive (Macintosh HD), Open Disk Utility (it may be under Launchpad depending on your OS X version, or you can use Spotlight by pressing Command + Space and typing in Disk Utility), and then choose "Repair Disk Permissions."

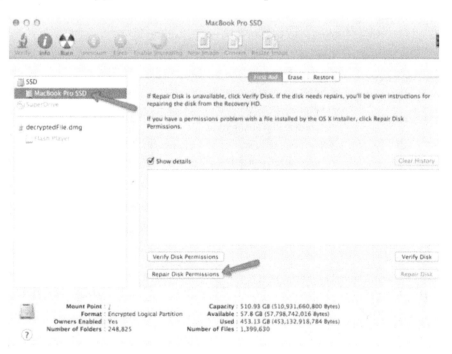

## 6. VERIFY AND REPAIR DISK

You may verify the integrity of the disk and file system using Disk Utility. In more current versions of macOS, Apple refers to that feature as "First Aid".

Usually, it shouldn't detect anything incorrect, but if it does, you need to correct it. To do this, you must first boot into what is known as Recovery Mode. Holding down the Command + R keys during the restart will cause your Mac to enter Recovery Mode when the Apple logo shows.

Open Disk Utility after entering the recovery console, pick the main hard disk of your machine, and then choose Repair Disk or First Aid based on your macOS/OS X version.

## 7. RESET SAFARI AND CLEAR CACHES

Note: The ability to reset Safari is no longer available on more current macOS versions.

After clicking on Safari to clear all of its caches, launch the browser and choose "Reset Safari..." from the menu in the top left corner of the screen. I'm using Safari 6, so you may need to go to Preferences to remove all caches on an earlier version.

If you use a different password manager (like 1Password), you may wish to deselect "Remove saved names and passwords" or make a backup copy of your passwords before deleting anything.

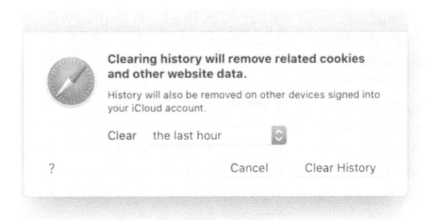

In later macOS versions, you may still choose Safari > Clear History to remove all of Safari's caches. Alternatively, you may remove website data from certain web sites by going to Safari > Preferences > Privacy > Manage Website Data.

### 8. CREATE A NEW USER ACCOUNT

In the rare event that there are problems with your user profile, creating a new user account is the recommended line of action. This is obviously an invasive process, since you risk losing settings and preferences. I consider this to be almost the final choice as a consequence. It's crucial to note, however, that I utilize this approach often to assess whether or not an issue is related to my user account. If it isn't, there's no need to go to the trouble of creating a new user.

To create a new user account, open System Preferences and choose Users & Groups. After selecting the lock symbol at the bottom of the screen, click the plus sign. Follow the on-screen directions to establish a new account.

## ROUTINE MAC MAINTENANCE TIPS TO KEEP YOUR SYSTEM OUT OF TROUBLE

### LEARN HOW TO BACK UP YOUR DATA

Data backup should always be your first concern. Not even Macs are unbreakable. If you have no backup strategy and anything goes catastrophically wrong, all of your hard work and precious images are gone forever.

But enough of the gory details. Mac's built-in Time Machine regularly backs up all of your data to an external drive so they can be readily recovered.

To set up Time Machine on your MacBook or iMac, you need to connect an external hard drive. Scheduling backups is this easy:

- • From the Apple menu, choose System Settings > General > Time Machine.
- • Click to choose the disk.

- • After choosing your disk from the list, click Use Disk. In the event that your Mac has not yet been setup for Time Machine, you may need to select Add Backup Disk and follow the prompts on the screen.

After that, Time Machine will start to make backups every hour for the last 24 hours, daily for the last month, and weekly for every preceding month. It is possible to retrieve objects from the Time Machine by accessing the corresponding window. For example, if you accidentally erased an email, open the Mail program. Click the Time Machine button (the little clock symbol) and then use the timeline to locate the required item.

## CLEAN UP JUNK FILES

If you're using a more recent version of macOS, make use of Mac's Optimized Storage function. It reduces clutter, automatically emptys the trash, improves storage by erasing previously seen TV series and movies, and moves some data to iCloud.

For best results, try to keep at least 10% of your disk space free at all times. This may be accomplished by regularly cleaning your PC of superfluous files.

- Click on Settings > General > Storage from the main Apple menu.
- Select Recommendations by navigating to the colored bar.

Junk may be swiftly found in several categories here. For a fast start, choose Applications and arrange them by Last Accessed.

Both will help you free up space rapidly, but neither offers a complete cleansing. Moving the primary app or item file is all that happens when you transfer an item to the trash. Cache and preference files are examples of connected trash that is ignored and takes up space on your system.

## REMOVE THOSE MYRIADS OF DESKTOP ICONS

Every program, file, and desktop snapshot need RAM from Mac. Consequently, the more items you put on there, the more system resources it consumes. To keep your desktop clear of clutter, use CleanMyMac X to eliminate everything you don't need from it and organize objects into folders.

## UTILIZE THE STACKS FUNCTION.

This began with Mac OS Catalina. One of the fundamental features for organizing is stacks.

- On your desktop, right-click a blank area.
- Select, Use Stacks.

# CHAPTER FOUR
# OPTIMIZING PRODUCTIVITY

**M**any of us take great care when furnishing our home offices to encourage comfortable and effective work—I know I've spent hours choosing my desk top, carpeting, and other details. During this process, we sometimes forget to give our laptops the same care and attention. Your Mac is as much of a "office space" as your physical desk since it's the gateway through which you do all of your work. It is thus important that you try to adjust and optimize it for efficiency.

Since our brains require a lot of energy processing visual input, I learnt as a professional musician not to practice in front of the mirror too often since it uses up too much "brain juice". Seeing myself perform lessens my capacity to discern what actually counts, which is the sound I'm generating on my instrument.

In a similar vein, computers routinely display meaningless images to humans. We can do away with intrusive interface components and screen clutter since we don't need as much visual input as other sorts of workers.

Here, I'll suggest several apps to cover the holes in macOS's built-in capability along with a few odd, simple adjustments to help you get more done more quickly.

## 1. USE THE FOCUS FEATURE

In macOS Mojave, you may filter your alerts using the Focus feature. I have a focus I put up specifically for this reason, which allows me to only be contacted during work hours by my Zapier colleagues and emergency contacts. I've also created up Focuses (Foci?) for practicing music, working out, and sleeping.

For those of us with iPhones, your Mac's Focuses configuration will be instantly mirrored on your phone, allowing you to manage your alerts. I want to start by praising this native feature since it has made a big difference in my ability to concentrate. It's great to see Apple considering how long we can focus.

## 2. CREATE SEPARATE USERS

When using computers at home and at work, think about creating separate user accounts. You may, for example, just use your business account to join into Slack and your personal user to sign into Messages in order to keep things separate. To allow speedy switching, make sure that each user has a customized fingerprint set up in System Preferences > Touch ID.

## 3. USE KEYBOARD SHORTCUTS

Because you have to constantly move your hand from your keyboard to your mouse and back, there is a little but noticeable time loss, which reduces the input efficiency of trackpads and mice.

As a Customer Champion at Zapier, I utilize Zendesk shortcuts all day long to keep my fingers on the home row and my focus on our customers instead of on my computer. There are keyboard shortcuts for almost every software you use, including Zoom and Gmail. To progress, you may even create your own shortcuts or utilize an application like Keyboard Maestro.

If you find that tapping the command key is hurting your pinky too much, you can easily swap the command and caps lock keys on your Mac keyboard under System Preferences > Keyboard > Modifier Keys.

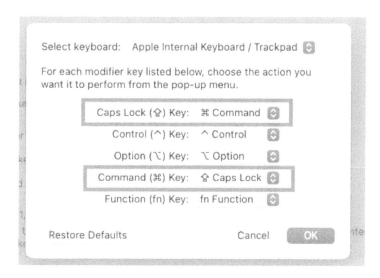

## 4. CLEAN UP YOUR DESKTOP

Consider not using your desktop at all. In desktop environments, there's an incomplete answer to a long-standing problem with multitasking (more on this later). That's why I advise against utilizing icons or folders on your desktop. For this reason:

If there are no icons on your desktop, it will seem less visually crowded overall.

If you don't have icons on your desktop, you'll need to make good use of your home folder and actively organize items.

If your desktop is empty of icons, then apps don't need to fight for screen real estate.

If you need to drag and drop files, example, into an email or from a web page to save, use a Finder window instead.

Try out a desktop backdrop that isn't a wallpaper while you're at it. To begin with, it isn't visually distracting. However, it also reminds me that when I sit in front of my computer and see a blank page, I am here to create, not to consume. Videos and beautiful pictures may wait till after work.

## 5. DON'T USE DOCK

Consider this a brazen plug if you don't use Alfred. I use it for a ton of other things, including password recovery and snippets. Alfred's basic but often overlooked feature is its ability to open programs immediately just by entering the name of the app and using your keyboard shortcut. If you think it would be too much effort, give it a go and note how much screen real estate the macOS Dock takes up, how long it takes for it to come back when hidden, and how much time you spend using the mouse to find programs.

- Please just hide your Dock: Dock & Menu Bar > Preferences > System Dock need to be shown and concealed automatically.

TinkerTool is another fantastic free program that allows you to turn off certain unused macOS visual components. In particular, think about turning off the Dock and Launchpad automations. In the unlikely event that you need to use these items immediately, you'll be shocked at how much more responsive they are after being deactivated.

## 6. REMOVE MENU BAR AND TOOLBAR ICONS

Toolbars with resizable icon sets are a feature of many native macOS programs. These symbols may take up a lot of space, especially in Finder and Apple Mail. To fully deactivate the toolbar, think about deleting all of its icons, or at the very least, switching them out for clickable text. Besides optimizing the visual environment, this will encourage the use of keyboard shortcuts.

I use Bartender to control the icons on my menu bar. The ability to choose when menu bar icons are shown is one feature that I really like using, especially Show for Updates. These are the standards that I've established:

- The battery symbol will only show up if the battery is less than 40% charged.
- Just show the Wi-Fi symbol when not connected to a network.
- When not connected to a VPN, only then will the VPN icon be shown.
- Generally speaking, just show the data in the menu bar of your Mac that you must always view. You may always click inside Bartender to go forward.

## 7. MANAGE YOUR WINDOWS

With several monitors and ultrawide screens these days, it's easy to become lost in a sea of open programs and overlapping windows. We're not very good at multitasking, so I've got to reevaluate how I screen properties while working.

I'll provide some bold recommendations here, the most crucial of which may be window management. Many of us easily snap or split windows using apps like BetterSnapTool or Magnet. Both of them are great, but the user has to decide how to set up the windows on the screen. If you are like me and find that running more than two or three programs at once is too much, try a tiling window manager. On the Mac, I use Amethyst. These are the things it does:

When I run an application on my desktop, it instantly maximizes to fill the screen. Distinct from a Mac application that is in "full screen" mode, which results in the application vanishing from your desktop.

When you run another app, your applications automatically adjust to fill half of your screen, left to right, creating a vertical split. Because dividing the screen vertically generates two places with a 4:3 aspect ratio—a very comfortable size for utilizing web apps—this works particularly well with ultrawide displays with a 21:9 aspect ratio.

When you launch a third app, the screen splits horizontally on the right side. Right now, the bottom half of my screen is taken up by the third app. If any of the applications are closed, the divides are immediately modified, and the other apps are automatically resized to cover the vacant area.

If you use this strategy, you'll never have to utilize Mission Control to search for overlapping windows again. Even better, Amethyst allows you to establish exceptions, so you can leave programs that need a tiny window floating and instantly go System Preferences to make changes when needed.

However, my method of managing windows is more intricate than that. To easily move between the six static desktops I've added to Mission Control, I configured the required keybindings in System Preferences > Keyboard > Shortcuts > Mission Control:

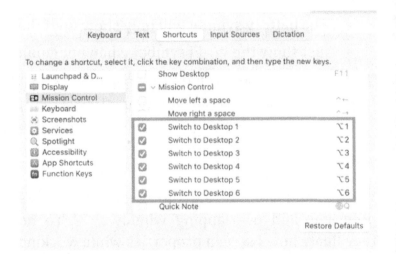

option #1: Proceed to the desktop

option #2: Proceed to desktop 2

option #3: Select desktop 3 (and so on).

(Tip: In Chrome, you may fast move between tabs by pressing command + the tab number. This provides a very fast method of navigating Mac desktops and browser tabs without ever using the mouse, in conjunction with the keybindings previously stated.)

Amethyst prefers bindings so that concentrated programs may be switched across desktops fast.

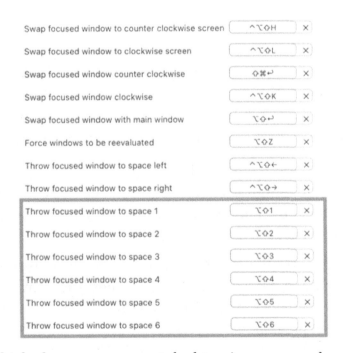

Shift + Option + desktop number> is how I operate.

In addition, I use a handy tool called SpaceId, which shows my current desktop in my menu bar.

My computer use has dramatically altered as a result of using Amethyst to manage my windows in this manner, saving me numerous mouse clicks. An unexpected bonus is that I no longer lose productivity when I forget to bring my ultrawide display. It's not any less pleasant to work on my 13" MacBook Pro screen since I always have other PCs ready to swiftly move to.

What my desktop computers would look like throughout a typical weekday:

- Desktop 1: When using my ultrawide monitor, Chrome splits into two windows on my first desktop.
- Desktop 2: To use a second Chrome window for customer service.
- Desktop 3: Slack.
- Desktop 4: Apple Music on.
- Desktop 5: Emacs (note-taking, to-do lists, and development learning) on desktop 5.
- Desktop 6: Firefox and Messages (personal apps.)

## 8. CLEAN UP YOUR BROWSER

I use Firefox for personal surfing, but Chrome is my go-to browser for everything work-related. I like having separate browser sessions since I don't want conflicts between my bookmarks, history, and logged-in accounts. With the wonderful program Choosy, you can choose which browser opens under certain conditions. Here are some of the settings I have made using Choosy as my preferred browser (instead of Chrome or Firefox) under System Preferences > General.:

- Always open links in Chrome when you click them in Slack.
- Always open links in Messages using Firefox after clicking on them.
- Ask me which browser to use when I access a URL from Alfred.

(And, yes, Choosy is compatible with Chrome profiles, before you ask.)

I would also consider removing the search suggestions in Chrome. I'm sure you're as organized about bookmarks as I am. But sometimes, it might be challenging to use the URL bar to find the right bookmark. To prevent Chrome from displaying pictures of car dashboards when you type a word like "dashboard," for example, you may wish to turn off Chrome's "Autocomplete searches and URLs" feature:

Chrome > Settings > Sync and Google services > Autocomplete searches and URLs.

Autocomplete searches and URLs

Sends some cookies and searches from the address bar and search box to your default search engine

The little changes I've suggested here are investments that will yield large returns down the road. Don't miss the opportunity to front-load extra enhancements that suit your particular working style. Most importantly, don't be afraid to simplify because you're an expert Mac user.

# CHAPTER FIVE

# EXPLORING MAC APPS AND SERVICES

t's possible that you are unaware that macOS has a Services menu item dedicated to applications. Services allow you to use a feature from one app without having to open it. Essentially, therefore, it's a method to get short cuts that enable you to do quick tasks. You have two options for creating shortcuts: create your own or use the ones that are currently there in the Services menu.

## HOW TO USE SERVICES

First, to find Services:

There are other options available, and you may use the Services menu whenever you'd want.

Open Safari, for example, and choose some text.

From the menu at the top, choose Safari. Then, scroll down to Services.

There are a lot of options displayed here. Some of the options may not be displayed depending on the installed programs and if you've changed your Services menu.

You may also access the services menu by right-clicking on the phrases that you have highlighted.

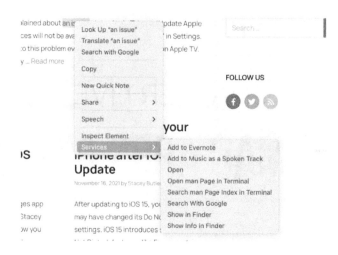

There are more Services available when you choose files. Choose the selected files on your desktop or in Finder, then click Finder from the top menu and go to Services to see what you can do with them.

## HOW TO CUSTOMIZE YOUR SERVICES MENU

In System Preferences, you may change the Services menu.

- You may choose and unchosen from the Service menu items that are now displayed
- Create keyboard shortcuts for the commonly used items.
- Create new Service menu items using Automator.

There are options in the Services menu that aren't compatible with every app. Certain products won't show up in the app's Services menu if you can't use them.

### SELECT/UNSELECT MENU ITEMS

- Choose System Preferences from the Apple menu. After selecting Keyboard, choose the Shortcuts tab.
- From the menu on the left side of the window, choose Services.
- It will show the whole Service menu. To see more, scroll down.
- To add an option, tick the box next to it. To remove it, uncheck the box.
- Each option is offered under a category, such Pictures, Messaging, and Development. You can make it easier to browse the options if you click the "carrots" next to the category heads to collapse that category.

### ADD KEYBOARD SHORTCUTS FOR SERVICES

For any option in the Services menu that you know you'll use often, you may set a keyboard shortcut. This will save you the trouble of having to navigate the menu each time you want to use the service.

- Under System Preferences > Keyboard > Shortcuts, services are shown in the list on the left.

Choose a service from the menu. The text "Add Shortcut" should appear next to the item. Select Shortcut to add it.

You should specify the keystrokes that you want to use for your keyboard shortcut.

The option to "Add Shortcut" may return after you input your shortcut. When you click Add Shortcut on this or any other item in the list, your shortcut key combination will appear next to the item.

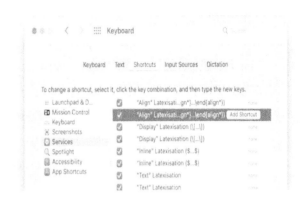

## CREATE NEW ITEMS USING AUTOMATOR

several guides on how to use Automator may be found online, along with several ideas for creating tasks that can increase your productivity. To change the type of files, close all active applications, or meaningfully rename a collection of files without changing each one individually, you may build an automation.

## ESSENTIAL MAC APPS

Since they are often less well-known, well-known Mac applications like Evernote, 1Password, Dropbox, Skype, OneNote, or Google Drive are not featured in our list of essential Mac apps. All of the applications on this page is also compatible with the latest macOS versions, Big Sur and Catalina.

Let's get going.

- Raycast is a powerful Mac Spotlight replacement that allows for quick application searches, web searches, and more. It is also possible to create custom processes using JavaScript.

- Think of Notion as a note-taking application that can also be used as a calendar, spreadsheet, wiki, to-do list organizer, and project management tool.

- Outlook is the best email app for Mac and no longer requires an Office license or a subscription to Microsoft 365. Spark is a good replacement for Apple Mail.

- With customizable keyboard shortcuts, Magnet is the perfect Mac window management program, enabling you to resize windows and drag and drop them. Windows may also be shifted across several monitors. There is still the option of rectangle.

- Setapp: a collection of upscale Mac tools and programs packaged together. Included are favorites like CleanshotX for screen capture and Capto for screen recording.

- Shottr: An artistic Mac program for taking and annotating screenshots that's easy to use. It is feasible to do both OCR and complete web page capture. I also use CleanShot X and Xnapper.

- ImageOptim - Make sure to run any photographs via ImageOptim before adding them to your website. The software will reduce the size of your picture files without compromising on quality.

- Warp—a modern alternative to the Mac Terminal. It's fast, beautiful, and equipped with AI search to convert spoken phrases into executable shell commands.

- Site Sucker: Store whole websites on your local computer, including with graphics and PDF files, so you can access them when offline. similar to wget but including a graphical user interface.

- App Cleaner: The greatest Mac uninstaller will automatically remove any unnecessary files that a program leaves on the hard drive.

- Maccy is a clipboard manager that saves whatever you copy to the clipboard and lets you paste copied text into other apps with a single shortcut. [CopyClip] is a worthy replacement.

- Clean Me: To free up space on your Mac, delete any temporary files, cache, and system logs that your machine can easily get rid of.

- Doodler is an excellent replacement for the well-known Bartender program. On the Mac menu bar, you may quickly rearrange or even hide the program icons.

# CHAPTER SIX

# CUSTOMIZATION AND PERSONALIZATION

With macOS, changing the interface's backdrop, colors, icons, audio, and other elements is easy. Make your Mac seem genuinely unique by personalizing the Dock, the notification sound, your profile image, and other settings that impact system functionality.

You may also make more detailed adjustments, change how apps look in Dark Mode, and set unique backgrounds for Finder windows using third-party tools. In the sections that follow, I'll walk you through some customization options for your Mac.

Over time, Apple has switched to a more straightforward user interface. MacOS works well right out of the box, while there is room for improvement. Customizing a few settings can enhance macOS's functionality for you.

You may simply customize your Mac's look and feel. Find out how to customize your Mac by changing the macOS settings to your liking.

# PERSONALIZING THE APPEARANCE ON YOUR MAC

Customizing a Mac to make it exclusively yours is helpful. There are even whole websites dedicated to Mac theming. Rather than use third-party tools for different looks, I'll show you what Apple can do.

For this session, I'll be using the most current version of the operating system, macOS 10.12 Sierra. Regardless of the version you are using, you will find that the basic concepts are the same with just little differences. Now let's play around with some enjoyable ways to change the look and feel of your Mac.

# 1. HAVE THE WALLPAPER CHANGE ON ITS OWN EVERY FEW HOURS OR DAYS.

The concept of desktop wallpaper as a metaphor for computers has never appealed to me. I guess changing the tablecloth doesn't feel the same.

- To change the wallpaper, go to System Preferences > Desktop & Screen Saver (or tablecloth). Use the Apple symbol located in the menu bar's upper left corner to go there, or use Command-Space to launch Spotlight and search for "Desktop" to find the option.

- Once you've selected a photo for the wallpaper, you may choose to have it change on its own. One may also customise how often the wallpaper changes. Click the check box in the Change Picture: box, then choose the appropriate interval from the drop-down menu.

- If you'd like, you may decide to have the backdrop pictures appear at random. Click the check box to toggle the Random order box to the on position.

- To keep things organised, save the background photos in an own folder in iPhoto. As long as the Desktop & Screen Saver window is open, you don't have to bother about adding one whenever you download anything new.

Alternatively, you may use any Mac folder that has a large number of photos in it.

## 2. TURN ON SCREEN SAVERS AND OTHER DEVICES WITH HOT CORNERS.

- To explore the available screen savers, click the Screen Saver tab in the Desktop & Screen Saver settings box. In the lower right corner, there is a Hot Corners button.
- By clicking on any of the four screen corners, you may carry out preset activities with the aid of the macOS system feature called Hot Corners. It could do a different action, such as launching a screen saver or opening LaunchPad or the Notification Center.
- Point the mouse cursor to the appropriate corner to activate a feature.

## 3. ADD SPACERS TO THE DOCK

A number of application icons may rapidly overwhelm the dock of your Mac. If so, adding a space between the symbols might help make greater sense of the circumstances.

This command generates translucent tiles that may be easily removed from the dock as needed.

- defaults write '{"tile-type"="spacer-tile";}'; com.apple.dock persistent-apps -array-add; killall Dock

To activate a blank tile, open Terminal and enter the following command:

After the command is executed, the dock will momentarily disappear and reload with an invisible tile to create a gap.

In order to provide room between icons, the invisible tile may be moved along the dock or deleted if it is no longer required.

## 4. MODIFY THE MAC OPERATING SYSTEM'S COLOR SCHEME

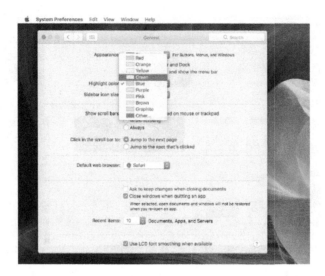

- If you would like a different color for highlighted text than the standard blue, go System Preferences > General and change the Highlight Color: option to that color.

- In addition to the eight possibilities in the menu, you may use the Other... option to choose any color from the color picker.

Graphite is an additional look option that changes the color of all program windows, menus, and buttons to a monochromatic style. This is for you if you like a very simple look without the eye-catching close, minimize, and zoom buttons on the window bars. It is only available in two colors: blue and graphite.

## 5. ADD DOCK MAGNIFICATION, HIDE IT, AND CHANGE ITS POSITION

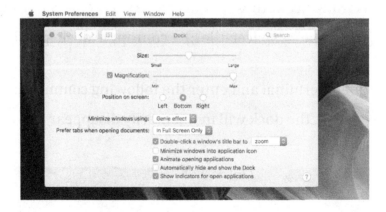

Unlike earlier Macs, the Mac's dock does not instantly draw your attention when it is first opened. The reason for this is because magnification has been turned off.

- To activate it, choose Dock by clicking the Apple symbol in the top left corner of the menu bar, and then click Turn Magnification On.

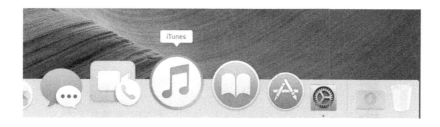

You may also choose to hide the dock from this option, which helps to optimize screen real estate, especially on small laptop displays. You may expose the dock by dragging the mouse to the region of the screen where it is hidden.

You have the option to reposition the dock to the left or right of the screen. The dock will seem differently if you move it to the sides; it will be more two-dimensional and like OS X 10.4 Tiger.

# HOW TO CUSTOMISE THE MENU BAR ON YOUR MAC

Usually, the menu bar isn't used to its maximum advantage. Though other applications use it for more information, there are some very creative things you can do with the data there. Let's look at some fantastic customization choices for the Mac Menu Bar.

## ADD SECONDS AND A DATE TO THE TIME

You may display more than just the time on the menu bar. Click the time now and choose Open Date & Time Preferences to expand. The main tab has a location where you may adjust the time and date.

If that's true, go directly to the Clock tab. Instead of using a digital display to represent the time in seconds, use analog time with flashing time separators. Use a 24-hour clock, make the AM/PM indicators visible or hidden, Show the workday. Every quarter, half, and hour, the time is announced and the current date is shown on the menu bar.

Many interesting time-related aspects of Mac OS are hidden. The date shown in the menu bar is significant, and if you want to be on time, seconds might be helpful. Keep in mind that you may change the date format in the Language & Text box. Later, I'll go into more detail.

## ADD BATTERY PERCENTAGE AND LIFE TIME

You must upgrade your portable Mac's battery indicator if it's only an icon in the menu bar in order to get more details. After plugging it in, click it and choose Show Percentage to get a reading charge. Next, disconnect the MacBook's charging adapter to see how things work.

Note: The ability to show the battery life left in the current mode was removed in Mountain Lion. whether you're using a previous version of OS X, click the battery icon to see whether there is that option.

# HOW TO SET PERSONAL PREFERENCES ON A MAC

Everyone likes to change things to suit their own circumstances. This is where you can find the fun little settings that you may make on your Mac.

## CHANGING THE ACTION ON INSERTING A CD OR DVD

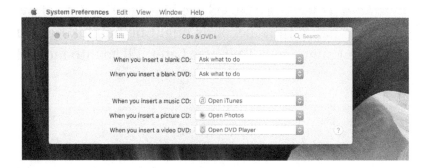

It's possible that you don't always want DVD Player to launch whenever you insert a disc into your Mac's video disc drive.

To change the behavior, open the CDs & DVDs tab in System Preferences. To alter a function, choose "Open other application..." by clicking on it. If you want to entirely deactivate the feature, choose Ignore.

You may even use Run Script if you have a custom function.

## ADJUST WHAT SPOTLIGHT SEARCHES AND HOW IT'S ORDERED

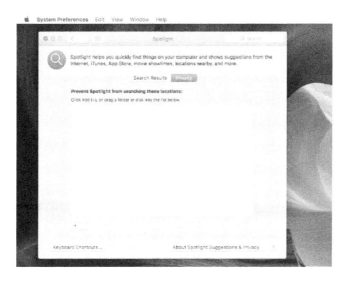

It's possible that the search results shouldn't include any of your private files. If so, you may exclude them from a system-wide Spotlight inquiry. Here's how it works:

• Launch System Preferences and click Spotlight

• Tap the Privacy tab

• To add a folder or an entire disk that you do not wish to be visible, click the Add button.

You may also modify the way Spotlight displays the search results. On the Search Results page, deselect the categories you don't want to see and rearrange them in the desired order. Here's where you may change the Spotlight shortcut as well.

## CHANGE THE DEFAULT DICTIONARY ON YOUR MAC

Apple's Dictionary app is among the most useful programs on the Mac. It works well and is simple to use.

But if you're like me, you would much rather look up words in the British dictionary—a true English dictionary. To activate a different language, open the Preferences window and check the box next to the language you want displayed in the main window of the program.

The Apple dictionary and Wikipedia, two of the ten dictionaries and thesauruses that come with the Mac, are more resources than dictionaries.

## CHANGE APP ICONS ON YOUR MAC

If you're that serious about customizing and making things your own, you can even alter the program icons on your Mac. On a Mac, updating an app's icon manually is a pretty straightforward job, however there are tools for this.

- Look up and download an icon on the internet. If the file is a standard.icns file, there won't be any issues with the next step.

- To see the file, choose the.png or.jpeg icon and open Preview. Select All from the Edit menu to make a duplicate of the selection. Regular.png files don't work since their backgrounds aren't always transparent.

- Find the program you want to modify, select it, and click Get Info. The keyboard shortcut Command-I is another option.

- To paste the new icon, click the little icon in the upper left corner of the application and press Command-V.

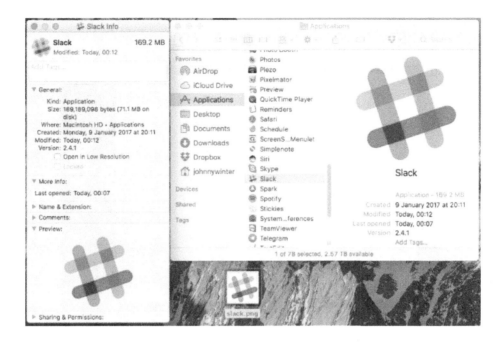

- To remove the little custom icon from the Get Info window, select it and use the Delete key on your keyboard.

manually: Apple's own applications were unable to work with this manner, however the majority of programs did.

## MAKE FINDER OPEN IN A DIFFERENT FOLDER THAN ALL MY FILES

On new Macs, the All My Files directory is shown by default when you launch Finder.

In my opinion, it is unacceptable. Fortunately, there is a way to change it.

- Navigate to the General tab in the Preferences of Finder.
- Choose a folder from the drop-down menu located under the New Finder windows.
- Choose Other to access any folder on your hard drive.

# SET REGIONAL VARIATIONS ON YOUR MAC

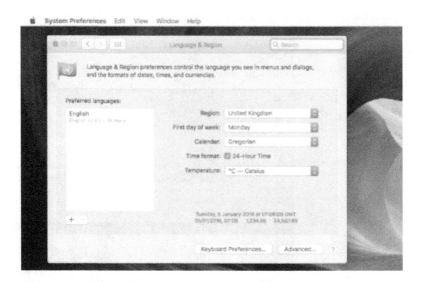

In the United States and other countries throughout the world, there are differences in the date format. Think about changing the format to something more reasonable, such descending YYYY-MM-DD or ascending DD-MM-YYYY. The latter is governed by an ISO standard. Spreadsheets in the ISO format, for example, could be sorted correctly.

- There's no need to format the date the same as the rest of the United States. You may alter that and other settings in the System Preferences Language & Text window. When you reach the Region tab, click on it. For you, here are some options:

- Let the Week Start on Any Day –Perhaps you would like for the week to start on Monday. Choose the day from the drop-down menu next to "First day of the week" to mark the beginning of the week.

- Select Customize next to the Dates section and rearrange the elements as necessary to change the date format. Apple made things pretty easy, so you can drag and drop the numbers and arrange them anyway you please. If desired, one may also mention the period, AD.

- Modify the time format so that milliseconds are included. Apple provides you with an option in the Customize screen under the Times section. Again, it is a drag-and-drop process.

- Modify the currency separators and decimal characters. There are others who would rather have commas and commas points as the decimal characters. If you fit that description, you may change the settings by selecting Customize located under the Numbers section. Any character may be substituted for the values.

- Modify Your Currency or Measurement Unit: You may modify the measurement unit and currency that you are currently using. The only accessible measurement systems are metric, US, and UK, despite the fact that there are several currencies. The UK is unique in this sense as it uses both imperial and metric measures.

# HOW TO CUSTOMIZE YOUR MAC FINDER

You ought to take possession of the macOS file browser. Let's look at how to customize it and some entertaining features that come with your Mac Finder.

## ORGANISE YOUR FOLDERS AUTOMATICALLY

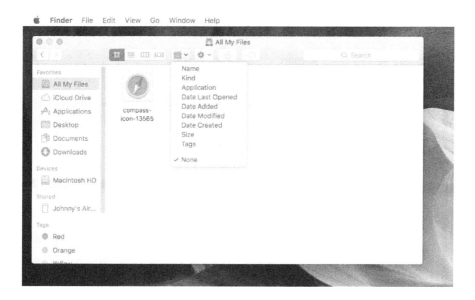

It irritates me when a folder is completely changed due to poor organization. For these kinds of objects, there are settings in the Finder toolbar.

- Click the button that looks like a small selection of icons, as seen in the screen shot above, to choose the organizing technique that works best for you. Names are the best to use since they are always present in the right location.

- On the other hand, you have complete control over Kind, Size, and Label. Alternatively, you may mix things up a little by moving items off the grid.

## REMOVE MOUNTED DISCS FROM THE DESKTOP

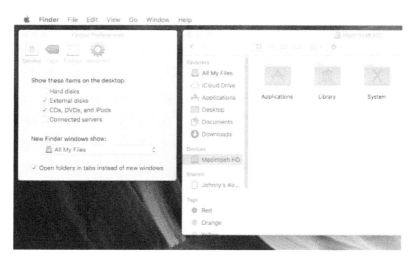

Perhaps you don't want an external hard drive or a CD taking up space on your desktop.

> Select the General tab after opening Finder's Preferences. Uncheck the option to display these items on the desktop.

That will clear off some                                              clutter on the desktop.

## BRING BACK THE STATUS BAR

A status bar at the bottom of the Finder window used to show the size of a selection, the number of files in a folder, and other pertinent information.

It was turned off by default in OS X 10.7 Lion, however you can always turn it back on using the easy keyboard shortcut Command / (Command Oblique).

Select Display Status Bar from the View menu as an option.

# CHAPTER SEVEN

# ENHANCING MULTIMEDIA EXPERIENCE

I n the post-lockdown age, video conversations are becoming an essential part of daily life. Businesses use them for planning meetings, societies use them for planning, and families use them for catch-up. This demand can be lessened and the quality of your interaction improved with an excellent video conference.

Despite the ease of use and simplicity of macOS's volume and sound settings, some users may want further control over the audio on their Mac.

But, some people may not find video calling on their Macs to be a pleasant experience. Occasionally, you may be able to fix the issues by yourself that might cause your video conversations to become less clear. To help you improve the audio and visual quality of your calls, I've put up a list of changes you should think about making.

# ADJUSTING THE SETTINGS FOR VIDEO CALLING APPS

Many of the apps we use cater to a broad range of customers with varying degrees of internet reliability, therefore many developers make sure their video call programs can adjust call quality as required. Although this is a good thing, you could get bothered by it if any of these qualities negatively affect you. I've included tips on how to improve the sound quality of calls on a few popular programs.

## FACETIME

Compared to other apps, FaceTime doesn't provide as many customizable options. Still, there are a few things you may turn on to potentially enhance your screen.

One of these features, available in macOS Monterey (and later versions), is Portrait mode, if your Mac is built with Apple silicon. This option enhances your face by distorting your surroundings to draw attention to you.

To turn on Portrait mode, follow these instructions:

- When in the midst of a FaceTime video chat, access the Control Center via the menu bar.
- In the top left corner, under Video Effects, choose Portrait.
- You may deselect it by choosing it again with the Portrait button.

## USE AN EXTERNAL WEBCAM

A MacBook may not be enough if you want the newest movies for your video chats, particularly if you have a MacBook Air, which only has a 720p camera (unless you get the 2022 model with the M2 CPU).

This problem can be fixed because, while built-in cameras are frequently smaller and have inferior electronics, external cameras are always superior. Investing around $100 on a high-quality 1080p camera will help you capture better videos.

Remember to change the app's settings after connecting your external device so you can use the camera.

## USE YOUR IPHONE AS A WEBCAM

If your iPhone is running iOS 16 or later and your Mac is running macOS Ventura or later, you may utilize the Continuity Camera function. Your Mac's webcam could soon be replaced by the primary camera on your iPhone.

The fact that Continuity Camera does away with the need for a second external camera is very great. Furthermore, the iPhone's camera is better than most webcams. It's also wifi and boasts a host of unique features, such Desk see, which allows you to see your desk's contents and your face at the same time.

## TURN OFF THE AUDIO VOLUME POPS

Most Mac users are probably used to the popping sound that plays whenever the keyboard's volume control keys are pressed. This indicator, which is meant to represent how loud or quiet the system audio will be if left at the previously selected setting, is not to everyone's taste.

In the macOS settings menus, after selecting the volume control in the menu bar, you may choose the Sound Preferences... option to permanently stop pops. Alternatively, choose the Apple logo, Sound, and System Preferences from the menu bar.

Under the Sound Effects tab, uncheck the box next to the Play feedback when volume is adjusted option.

There is also a short-term way to disable the pop sound effect if you would want the audio confirmation to stay on. Holding down the Shift key while tapping the volume adjustment keys on the keyboard can muffle the popping noises; releasing the key will cause the popping sounds to restart.

## FINER VOLUME ADJUSTMENTS

Arguably the most popular way to change the volume on a keyboard is to use the volume keys. This method only provides 16 different sound output levels (or 17 if you include silence), and sometimes you want to adjust the volume to be in the middle of the two.

The simple way to do this is to use the menu bar icon to change the volume if the icon is enabled in the Sound settings. If it's not in the menu, you may fast change the volume by pressing the volume control keys on the keyboard and holding down Option-Shift at the same time.

When this key combination is used, in addition to mute, there are 64 volume settings available, and the volume control buttons now adjust the volume in quarter-step increments. It should be noted that if the volume is set to a quarter- or half-step, hitting the volume keys will immediately boost the volume to the next full step without the need for additional modifier keys.

More to the point, the same method works for the keyboard's brightness settings as well; the Option-Shift modifier again divides the adjustment into quarter steps.

## AUDIO INPUT SELECTION

A list of audio outputs may also appear in the menu bar when you pick the volume icon if your Mac is linked to many sound-producing devices and accessories. This does not apply to audio inputs, but it does allow users to quickly set up an alternate audio output (e.g., using speakers from a connected display instead of the Mac or MacBook speakers).

When you click the volume icon while holding down Option, the audio output options will pop to the top and the volume control slider will vanish. The menu will display all of the Mac's audio inputs that are presently in use while emphasizing the chosen input, rather than outputs.

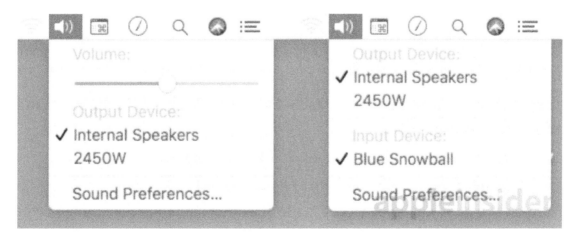

In the same way that you may alter the outputs, selecting a different input from this menu will switch to that particular device.

# CHAPTER EIGHT

# REACHING NEW HEIGHTS WITH MACBOOK ACCESSORY

# ESSENTIAL ACCESSORIES FOR THE MACBOOK

THE MACBOOK is a powerful computer. Whether you're using a MacBook Air for emailing and web browsing or a MacBook Pro for more visually intensive jobs like video editing and 3D modeling, Apple laptops are capable of handling a wide range of tasks. But to enhance your experience, I suggest adding a few extras.

A range of accessories, including as external displays, charging bricks, laptop stands, and keyboards, may be coupled with your MacBook, regardless of the model you pick or the purpose for which you're using it. The items in the above list are the best MacBook accessories for optimizing your computer's performance and streamlining your workflow. Since there are many attachments, this is by no means an exhaustive list.

## CHARGING ADAPTERS

Despite the fact that MacBooks now have longer battery lives, you should always carry an extra charger. The huge one that is included in the bundle is limited to charging one device at a time.

## LAPTOP CASES AND SLEEVES

Scratching or denting the metal casing of a MacBook is rather easy. Investing in a laptop sleeve or cover is a wise move to protect it.

- Incase Hardshell Case Dots for MacBook Pro 16-inch model.
- Speck Smartshell Case for MacBook Pro 14-inch model.
- A MacBook Magnetic Envelope Sleeve made of leather: the Harber London Magnetic Sleeve.

## HUBS AND DOCKS

If the limited number of ports on your MacBook Air or older MacBook Pro bother you, get a USB hub or dock. The cheap dongles called hubs have a headphone jack, SD card readers, and extra

USB ports. Docks are intended to be used at a desk because they are larger, have more ports in more varieties (like Ethernet), and occasionally have their own power source.

- Twelve South StayGo Mini
- Plugable USB-C Triple Display Docking Station

## IF YOU HAVE AN IPHONE

Anker 637 Magnetic Charging Station

Are you attempting to discard the desk power strip? You need look no further than Anker's MagGo 637. Your iPhone can be charged wirelessly from the front MagSafe charger, and it has three AC outlets, two USB-C connectors, and two USB-A ports on the back. With a 65 watt output, you can use one of those USB-C connections to charge a MacBook, turning it into a compact, all-in-one charging station.

## KEYBOARDS

If you work a lot at a desk, it's great, but not necessary, to spend extra money on a better keyboard. particularly if you prefer a more tactile experience with a mechanical keyboard.

- Apple Magic Keyboard with Touch ID and Numeric Keypad
- Logitech MX Mechanical Mini for Mac

## MOUSE

A good mouse is necessary to provide the most pleasant experience possible. I have an external trackpad and an ergonomic option (to reduce wrist strain) for you if you really value the trackpad on your MacBook.

- Logitech Lift for Mac
- Apple Magic Trackpad 2

## LAPTOP STANDS

By placing your MacBook on a laptop stand, you can prevent craning your neck to look at the screen.

- ObVus Solutions Laptop Tower Stand
- Nnewvante Laptop Stand

## DESK MATS

Although it looks wonderful, your workplace doesn't actually require a desk mat. It could also give the area a somewhat neater, more appealing appearance. They may also be used as a mousepad by anybody who uses an external mouse.

- Grovemade Wool Felt Desk Pad
- Satechi Dual-Sided Eco-Leather Deskmate

# EXTERNAL STORAGE SOLUTIONS AND BACKUPS

Upgrading the storage on Macs has never been easier, so purchasing an external drive to offer additional space for all of your corporate data, personal files, movies, and games is always a wise choice. An external drive should also be carried about at all times so that Time Machine backups may be made in case anything goes wrong.

Modern solid-state drives (SSD), which are remarkably tiny, durable, and speedy, are the greatest substitute. In comparison, a 4TB basic desktop hard disk with a USB interface may be bought for the same amount of money. Even with their recent price reduction, 1TB SSDs are still somewhat pricey (high-speed Thunderbolt drives are often more expensive). Hard drives are still the most affordable option if you need a lot of storage for your backups and important data, even if they are slower than SSDs.

There are other possibilities as well, such as tiny, portable hard drives designed for laptop usage and desktop drives with really large capacities if you really need a lot of storage. Integrated docks with multiple Thunderbolt and USB ports and the ability to open the disk's shell and swap out the drive inside for an instant upgrade are two other benefits that certain hard drives provide.

## SEAGATE ULTRA TOUCH 2023

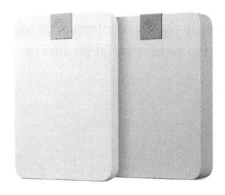

## PROS

- Competitive price
- 2TB, 4TB or 5TB storage
- Password protection and encryption

## CONS

- Average performance
- Larger and heavier than original model

## LACIE MOBILE DRIVE 2022

## PROS

- Competitive price
- LaCie's ToolKit app

## CONS

- Not the fastest hard drive available

# TIPS AND TRICK IN MAC OS SONOMA

## SCREEN SAVERS

Screen savers have changed from their original purpose of protecting outdated CRT monitors from screen burn-in to a fun and inventive way to customize your Mac experience. While burn-in problems are no longer a concern with contemporary screens, screen savers are still a fantastic way to show off beautiful images while your Mac is not in use.

**How to Use Screen Savers on macOS Sonoma**

Although using screen savers on a Mac is nothing new, Apple has entirely redesigned the process with macOS Sonoma. After updating to macOS Sonoma, the revamped Lock Screen will be the first thing you see when you connect into your account. Similar to what you would see on your iPhone or iPad, the different users will be displayed at the bottom while the date and time are displayed at the top.

1. Ensure that macOS Sonoma is the most recent version and is installed on your Mac.
2. On your Mac, launch the System Settings program.
3. Scroll down in the sidebar on the left and select Screen Saver.

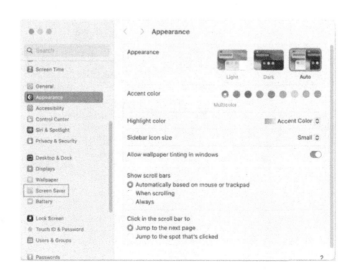

4. Find and choose a screen saver from one of the following categories that you wish to use:

**Landscape**

- Greenland
- Grand Canyon
- Hawaii
- Iceland
- Patagonia
- Yosemite

**Cityscape**

- New York
- Hong Kong
- London
- Los Angeles
- Dubai

**Underwater**

- Humpback Whale
- Palau Jellies
- Barracuda
- Palau Coral
- California Kelp Forest
- California Dolphins

**Earth**

- Caribbean Day
- Middle East
- Caribbean
- Nile Delta
- Iran and Afghanistan

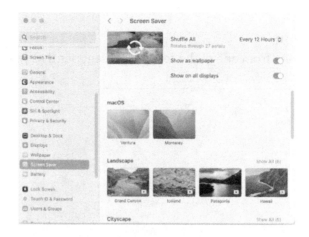

5. Once selected, your Mac will start downloading the specified screen saver. The amount of time left for the screen saver to download is indicated by a progress bar.

The option to set the image as your wallpaper is another great touch that Apple included with the launch of new screen savers in macOS Sonoma. If the picture has completed downloading, all you have to do is click the button next to Show as wallpaper to instantly change your backdrop.

Finally, you may individualize the screen saver for each linked monitor if your Mac has several displays. Alternatively, you may apply the screen saver to any connected monitors or displays by clicking the toggle button next to Show on all displays.

## How To Shuffle Aerials Screen Savers On MacOS Sonoma

The inclusion of Apple's selection of "Aerials" screen savers is one of the unnoticed additions in macOS Sonoma. These have been accessible on the Apple TV for a while, inspiring several developers to make programs that make the wallpapers available for the Mac. However, such workarounds are no longer required, and with macOS Sonoma, you may even mix the screen savers for Aerials. Ensure that macOS Sonoma is the most recent version and is installed on your Mac.

1. On your Mac, launch the System Settings program.

2. Scroll down in the sidebar on the left and select Screen Saver.

3. Reach the Shuffle Aerials section by scrolling down.

***Choose one of the following:***

- Shuffle All

- Shuffle Earth

- Shuffle Cityscape

- Shuffle Landscape

- Shuffle Underwater

1. Return to the page's top after choosing.

2. Shuffle All's drop-down menu should be selected.

***Choose one of the following:***

- Every Day

- Every Week

- Every 12 Hours

- Every 2 Days

- Every Month

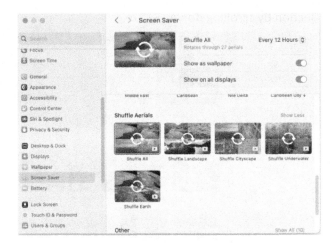

Screen savers are a simple and enjoyable way to customize your Mac and maximize your display while it is not in use. You should be able to configure and utilize screen savers on macOS after reading this article. Keep in mind that if you wish to experiment with a different appearance, you can always modify your screen saver settings.

# ADD WIDGETS TO YOUR DESKTOP

A widget is something that may simplify your digital life if you have utilized any mobile platforms in the past. You might include educational widgets that only keep you informed of the data you require.

Several of the programs you have installed on your laptop or desktop, such as Batteries, Calendar, Clock, Contacts, Drafts, News, Notes, Podcasts, and many more, may be used with interactive widgets. Many of the widgets are also available in a variety of sizes, with each offering a unique degree of information to convey.

Naturally, not everyone appreciates a good widget. However, MacOS Sonoma is prepared to serve them to those who do. Even better, the widgets will gradually fade away when you switch your attention to the programs, reducing the likelihood that they will divert you from what you are doing.

You may install as many widgets as your desktop can accommodate to sate your desire for instant access to information. Let's now look at adding widgets to your desktop. There is only one potential exception to the procedure's simplicity.

## How To Add Your First Macos Sonoma Widget

The only thing you'll need for this is a MacOS system running Sonoma, such a MacBook Pro or an iMac. You won't be able to install widgets if your laptop or desktop is running a version of MacOS older than Sonoma, so make sure to do the upgrade.

1. **Turn off Stage Manager**

I'll make the disclaimer right now. I quickly learned that in order to use the desktop right-click (or two-finger touch) menu if you use Stage Manager, as I do, you must first disable it. You may easily re-enable Stage Manager once you've added your widgets.

To turn off Stage Manager, click the icon in the Menu Bar and then drag the Stage Manager On/Off slider to the off position.

2.  Open the Widgets editor

Right-click (or two-finger tap) any empty space on the desktop while Stage Manager is deactivated, then select Edit Widgets from the popup menu.

3.  Add your widgets

Locate the widgets you wish to add in the Edit Widgets box, and then drag them to your desktop. Then, you may arrange them whatsoever and in whichever sequence you choose. Click Done once you're done.

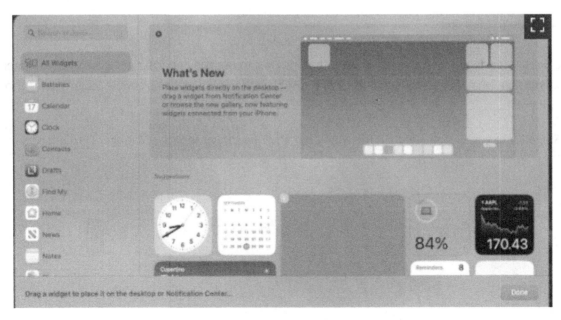

4. Enjoy your widgets.

Your desktop should now be partially or completely covered in educational and/or interactive widgets. Remember to go back and re-enable Stage Manager if you use it.

You only need to right-click (or two-finger touch) the widget you want to delete and choose delete Widget if you change your mind and want to get rid of it later.

The process of adding widgets to your MacOS Sonoma desktop is complete at this point. With these little improvements, Sonoma will prove to be a tremendous asset in helping you work more productively.

## WIDGETS FADE FOR BETTER FOCUS

On the Mac desktop, widgets provide a quick look at the status of a program or event you're interested in. The macOS Sonoma allows you add a variety of widgets on your desktop, like weather and reminders. However, having full-color widgets on your desktop may distract you from your job when you're using your Mac. And without even recognizing it, each distraction impairs your performance. Fortunately, you can avoid this simply changing the widget's settings on your Mac to Monochrome. Here is how to go about it. This section will demonstrate how to mute Widgets on your Mac Desktop to improve focus.

Steps On macOS Sonoma, the widgets fade for greater focus.

When you adjust this widget option, widgets will automatically adjust their color to match the Wallpaper so you can focus on your current job. How?

1.  **Access the Apple Menu. Choose System Settings**

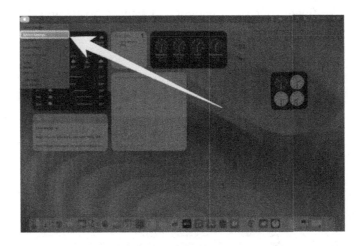

2.  Select Desktop & Dock on the left side.

3.  Swipe down to Widget Settings on the right side.

4.  Click the Widget Style Dropdown button now.

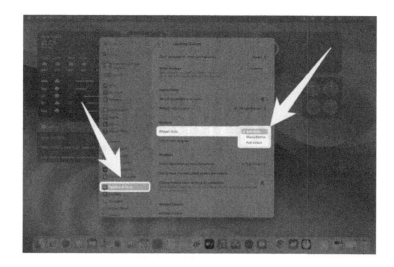

5. Finally, choose Monochrome. Get Widget Fade once and for all. Open any window on the screen, even if you are on your desktop.

It's done! Full-Color for Widget Style.

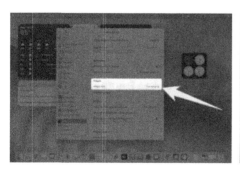

Final Thought!

For improved attention on macOS, you may do this by fading widgets. A widget for your iPhone may now be added to your Mac desktop with macOS 14.

# VIDEO CONFERENCING

New video conferencing tools from Apple have improved meetings on all platforms. Presenter Overlay, a feature of macOS Sonoma, enables users to overlay their own content on top of slideshows and other types of multimedia. They can choose to show up as a little bubble or a bigger frame.

The way the function operates is by putting the material in front of the participant and eliminating them from the background. According to Craig Federighi, Senior Vice President of Software Engineering at Apple, "macOS is the heart of the Mac, and with Sonoma, we're making it even more delightful and productive to use."

I believe buyers will adore macOS Sonoma and the fresh ways it gives them the ability to customize with widgets and gorgeous new screen savers, experience new levels of gaming performance, and gain incredible productivity for video conferencing and surfing with Safari.

Users may also have Reactions in other places, including adding confetti or virtual balloons to their call-related windows. These have the same design as Messages.  Hand gestures, like giving someone two thumbs up, will start the reactions, setting up a fireworks show behind the user. Any video conferencing software, such as Zoom, Microsoft Teams, and Webex, can have them enabled by users.

## PUT YOURSELF FRONT AND CENTER

If you have the proper camera, macOS Sonoma provides you Center Stage choices to choose how you display yourself to the world with new video conferencing tools like responses. The iPad version of Center Stage is exactly the same as the Mac. If you decide to enable it, the camera will automatically relocate if you reach out of the frame to get a coffee while you're on a video conversation.

In other words, it seems to. While there must be boundaries, your video conferencing coworkers will be able to see you in the center of their field of vision as long as you are in front of the camera someplace. In fact, they'll see you up front. The picture will automatically adapt to show the ideal framing whether you move to the left or right, up or down, or if someone else joins you in the photo.

***Center Stage has to be running on macOS Sonoma and be connected to an Apple Silicon Mac in order to:***

- a built-in camera, like the one found in a MacBook Pro

- Continuity using an iPhone 12 or later as a camera

Previously a component of Control Center, Center Stage now resides under a new menubar icon that now includes settings for portrait mode and responses. This new menubar symbol may really be blocked because it changes to show you whether your camera or merely your microphone is in use.

Currently, the yellow microphone or green camera indicator may be changed with a darker, less noticeable one if you were to utilize a screen-recording software while participating in a video conference call, just to provide one example. However, when you are on a video conference, the Center Stage controls will be located beneath this menubar icon.

## HOW TO USE CENTER STAGE IN MACOS SONOMA

- Click the new menubar icon while you are on the video conference.

- Click to activate Center Stage, or, if other options are available,

- click the arrow to the right of Center Stage to access them.

Center Stage was a Control Center checkbox in macOS Ventura. You may now turn it on or off by clicking the Center Stage symbol. There will be variations because your camera will affect a number of Center Stage's features. In contrast, macOS Sonoma offered more options than the identical configuration in macOS Ventura in AppleInsider testing utilizing an iPhone 13 Pro as the camera.

in particular, two choices. You could see a selection of cameras by clicking on the arrow to the right of Center Stage in the new menubar icon. If so, clicking will allow you to move between, say, Main and Wide Angle.

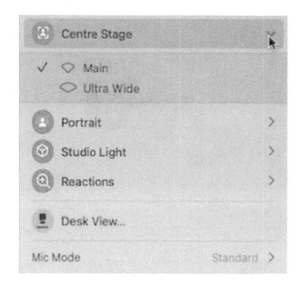

**A step forward in video conferencing**

On the Mac, Center Stage is just as welcoming as it was on the iPad. It's unfortunate that you can't activate it or deactivate it until you are really on a call. Prior to the other caller joining, you should be able to configure the call exactly how you wish. If it's your call and you're logged into Zoom, for example, you may start the conference and make changes before inviting anybody else. Instead of using the menubar icon, it would be convenient to be able to modify the settings with a keystroke or possibly a Shortcut.

## NEW SCREEN SHARING PICKER

The screen sharing picker is a new tool in the menu bar that helps you keep track of all your screen-sharing sessions in macOS Sonoma.

The screen sharing picker icon appears on the macOS status bar as soon as the DisplayLink Manager app has been granted screen recording permission (for more information on screen sharing permissions, please see macOS Sonoma 14: Screen Recording Permission).

When you click on the screen sharing picker icon in DisplayLink Manager 1.10 alpha or later, a menu will appear with a preview of each DisplayLink-enabled display, such as the one below

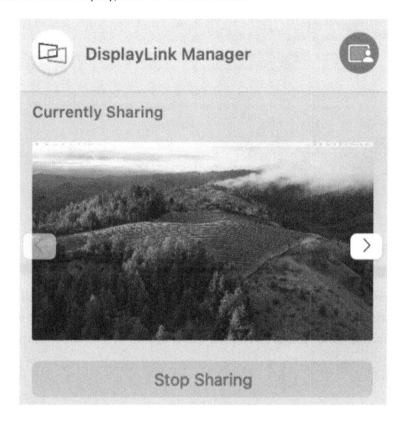

The arrow buttons let you switch between all of the display previews.

Additionally, there is a "Stop sharing" button in the picker menu's bottom section. If you click on it while previewing a screen that supports Displaylink, the screen recording session connected to it will end, which will cause your DisplayLink screen to become unresponsive (screen content will freeze).

The cease sharing button and the screen preview are hidden in DisplayLink Manager versions 1.9 and before. You must disable and enable the frozen display from the DisplayLink Manager app using the disable/enable toggle in order to restart your halted DisplayLink screen.

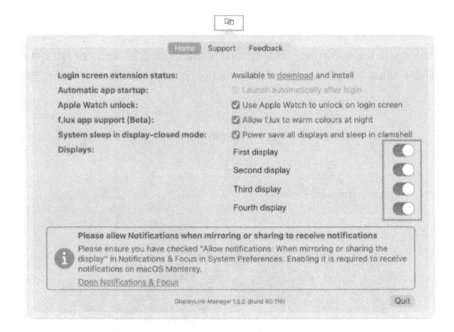

As an alternative, you can remove and replug the DisplayLink adapter/dock to automatically re-enable all connected DisplayLink-enabled monitors. If the screen sharing session you are in is the last one open when you click the "Stop sharing" button, an orange microphone symbol can momentarily appear in the macOS status bar.

The logo commonly refers to audio recording. In addition to being unable to record, DisplayLink Manager is also unable to send any video or audio back to Synaptics.

# SAFARI AND PASSWORDS

In macOS Sonoma, Apple has included a new Profiles feature to Safari that is intended to aid with privacy and focus while also making it simple to split surfing for work and home. Use it as follows.

Private browsing is a part of the new Safari Profiles feature, although it's actually more of a continuation of the concepts underlying Tab Groups and Focus Modes. It involves eliminating distractions so that you may pay attention to what you want to be doing at this precise moment.

Therefore, you may make a profile that is only for work. You can have a large selection of Tab Groups and even extensions in that Profile that are not present in any other Profile.

## CREATE A PROFILE

- Open Safari on your Mac.
- Select System Settings from the Safari menu.
- Click the Profiles button in the top row of the window that displays.
- Click New Profile on the information page that displays.

Only one of the options available in the New Profile window is necessary; the profile must have a name.

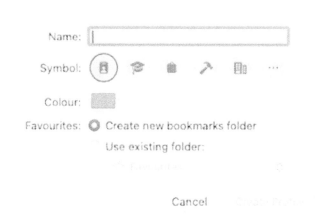

***In addition, you can decide to:***

- Decide on a profile icon.

- Decide on a color for it.

- a fresh bookmarks collection, or

- Use the Favorites folder you already have.

- then choose Create Profile.

Contrary to appearances, the color has more significance. After going through this, Safari will open in your new profile with that color as the backdrop when you open it for the first time.

When a color is applied to the whole Safari window, it might appear enormously intrusive even though it appears acceptable as a little thumbnail in the dialog box.

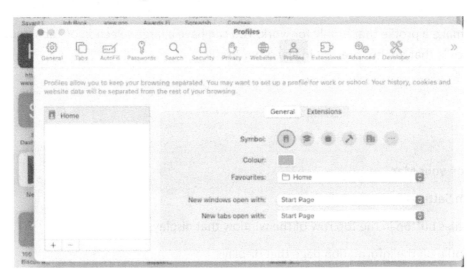

## FASTER AND MORE RELEVANT SEARCH

Similar to Chrome, Safari in Sonoma makes the process of creating profiles faster. So you can quickly do relevant searches. Apple claims that Safari's search is now quicker and offers "easier-to-read and more relevant suggestions."

## WEB APPS COME TO YOUR DOCK

Placing the websites you visit regularly right in the dock is a feature that is both practical and fascinating. You may simply add Gmail to your dock if, for example, you frequently use it and don't rely on the Mac's native email application. There are many things you may do, and it helps to avoid opening the website in the browser repeatedly. Remember that the site should have a PWA, or progressive web app, which is something that most websites often have.

To utilize the functionality, follow these procedures, The procedures listed below may be used to add websites to the dock in macOS Sonoma:

- Launch Safari.

- Visit the website you wish to include in the dock.

- In the menu bar, select File.

- the Add to Dock option.

- You may also give the website a new name and alter the symbol.

- Select Add.


Now the webpage should show up in the dock. Clicking the icon will open it. A website may be moved around and arranged whatever you wish once it has been placed to the dock. The webpage may be accessed in a new tab, new window, or full screen by selecting it with the right mouse button. Right-click on the icon and choose Remove from Dock to remove a website from the dock.

# MESSAGES

The Messages app will improve your search experience and give you the option to change it as you go. There will also be warnings about potentially sensitive content before you view the movies and pictures. A catchup for group conversations, an improved Sticker folder, and adjustments to Messages in iCloud will also be included in later updates.

## SEARCH FILTERS

Apple has updated the search functionality in its standard Messages app in iOS 17, iPadOS 17, and macOS Sonoma. You can now combine search queries and restrict results to quickly discover the messages you're searching for. Prior to iOS 17, you could enter a word or phrase in the Messages app's search area to get results that matched, but there was no mechanism to filter messages so you could locate what you were searching for more quickly.

For instance, you would have to search for "dinner" and then browse through a number of messages from anybody and everyone that had that phrase in order to find a message from a buddy named "John" that had the word.

Thank goodness, with iOS 17, you can now mix numerous filters. For instance, you may search for photographs from a certain person by typing "photos" and their name, then pressing to pick each search option to get more specific search results. Simple changes like this greatly improve the usability of the Messages app in iOS 17. Apple's most recent software update includes enhancements to the Messages app's other functions.

## A NEW WAY TO SHARE AND VIEW LOCATIONS

To let people know where you are, you can include your current location in a message. To share locations, both you and your recipients must be logged into iCloud. Additionally, Location Services must be enabled for Messages.

**Share your location**

- Choose a discussion in the Messages program on your Mac.
- One of the following actions can be taken after clicking the Info button in the top-right corner:
- One-time location transmission: To send my current location, click.

- The transcript includes a map that displays your present position. The map does not refresh when you change places.
- For an ongoing duration, share your location: Select the duration for sharing your location in the current chat by clicking Share My Location. For instance, you might share your location with someone till the end of the day, allowing them to see your current position at that time.

Stop sharing your location

- Choose a discussion in the Messages program on your Mac.
- Click Stop Sharing My Location after selecting the Info option in the top-right corner.

## CATCH-UP AND SWIPE TO REPLY

Swipe to respond is becoming a common feature in messaging applications. It makes it simpler to avoid misunderstandings during talks by allowing you to respond to a specific message in group or one-on-one chats.

The inline responses function was added by Apple to Mac with the release of macOS Big Sur in 2020. Nevertheless, in order to reply to a message, you had to right-click it and choose "reply."

But now that Apple has released upgrades for iOS 17 and macOS 14 Sonoma, it has finally caught up to other texting services. Now within the Messages app on your iPhone and Mac, you can just swipe to reply. On the iPhone, using this feature is simple and uncomplicated, but understanding how to utilize the swipe-to-reply functionality on a Mac computer may be a bit challenging.

I'll go over all you need to know about this function in this section and demonstrate how to use swipe to reply in Messages on Mac in macOS 14 Sonoma. Consequently, let's begin:

### Swipe to Reply in Messages on Mac in macOS 14 Sonoma

Prior to macOS 13 Ventura, you had to right-click the message and choose the Reply option in order to reply to a particular message. Despite the fact that this technique is still accessible in macOS 14 Sonoma, the addition of swipe to reply makes it more simpler and more efficient.

1. Open the Messages app on your Mac by selecting it from the dock or Launchpad. As an alternative, you may open the Messages app via the Spotlight Search function by pressing the shortcut keys Command + Space.

2. Start a discussion with your buddy in the Messages app once you've opened any chat where you wish to respond to a message.

3. Put the pointer on the message you wish to respond to, then use two fingers to swipe right on the trackpad.

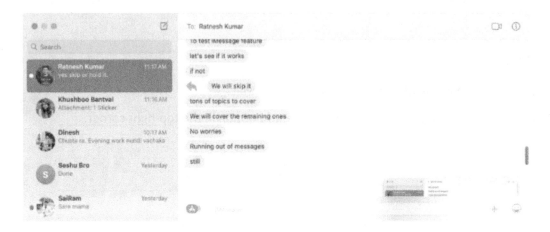

4. You may now respond to the message by pressing the return key to submit your response.

Swipe to respond in Messages is my favorite new feature in all of macOS 14 Sonoma, even if it joins a host of others like Presenter Overlay, Desktop Widgets, Web applications, and many others. If you enjoy this feature as well, please consider telling other Mac users about it and showing them how to respond to messages in style!

## ALL YOUR STICKERS IN ONE PLACE

Stickers are a tremendously fun method for us to express ourselves and improve the quality of our talks. Chat stickers are a more effective way than words to express sentiments, responses, and emotions. Apple seemed to concur with this as well.

If you've been following the iOS 17 and macOS 14 improvements since they were announced, you presumably know that Apple concentrated on Phone, FaceTime, and Messages for this year's releases.

Particularly intriguing new features for the Messages app include Check In, Search Filters, Swipe to Reply, Audio Transcriptions, Live Stickers, and more! This article will explain how to access stickers on Mac in macOS 14 Sonoma, even though I have previously written a separate guide on how to make and transmit Live Stickers on iOS 17. Having stated that, let's avoid the small chat and get to the point.

**Access Stickers on Mac in macOS 14 Sonoma**

It's crucial to remember before we continue that you can only access and send stickers from your Mac. You must use an iPhone to generate stickers if you wish to do so.

You may quickly access and send stickers you've made on your iPhone using your Mac after first making them on your iPhone. In macOS 14 Sonoma, use these steps to obtain stickers:

1. Open the Messages app on your Mac by selecting it from the dock or Launchpad.

2. Search for or launch the conversation you wish to exchange stickers with.

3. Next, click the Apps symbol that is right next to the text area.

4. From here, simply click on Stickers.

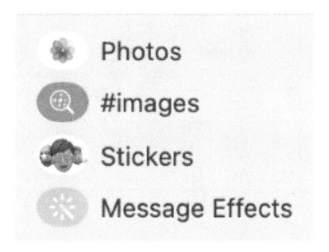

When you access the stickers, the Recent tab will by default be displayed. Do not worry if you cannot see your stickers there.

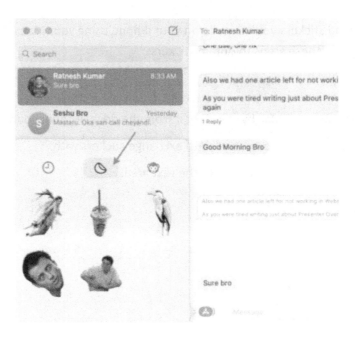

You may access all of the stickers you've made with your iPhone by selecting the Live Stickers option. In the third tab, you may also discover your Animoji stickers.

There you have it, then! In macOS 14 Sonoma, here is how you may access stickers on your computer. Simply click on the stickers to use them in your chat. You may use the trackpad to click and hold on the sticker and then drag it right into the messages you wish to respond to using stickers to give your chat more flair.

# PDFS AND NOTES

Apple Notes is a great location to keep all kinds of information, from a shopping list you'll later erase to everything you need for study. Apple now lets you link two or more notes together in macOS Sonoma so you can easily choose between ones that are linked.

You only see the improvements to PDFs once you're within a note. The usage of PDFs in Apple Notes is drastically improved by a few minor adjustments to how they are presented and subsequently edited.

**Store more PDFs in a note**

Apple emphasizes how helpful this is on its macOS Sonoma preview website. Keep many PDFs in a single note for quick access to related files. But in reality, there was nothing keeping you from adding many PDFs to a single letter; you simply didn't do it very often since it was inconvenient. For example, the PDFs were placed vertically and required endless scrolling whether there was only one PDF or several.

You might also choose View as Small Images from the context menu when you right-click on a PDF in your note. As a result, every PDF was instantly converted into a little graphic that actually consisted of just one icon and some text.

**Problems with collating and reading PDFs in Notes**

this view of condensed images did make it feasible to use an Apple Note as a collection of PDFs that are just organized as a set of icons. When you changed one back from an icon to a full PDF, you also turned back all of them, so you couldn't easily view them all.

You had to click on a PDF that was stored in Notes in order to open it in Apple's Preview app and view more than the first page.

It was possible to read a PDF while remaining in Notes, but you had to realize that the app's Markup capability was hidden beneath an icon in the PDF's upper right corner. When you right-clicked, other controls were accessible, but not this one.

Markup may be selected by clicking the simple-to-miss symbol with a downward-pointing arrow. The entire PDF then opened in a new Apple Notes window with all of its pages scrollable for easy reading.

Simply said, you couldn't read two together, and accidentally annotating a document may modify it significantly.


**SMALL BUT WELCOME MOVES**

Because they impact every action you take with a PDF in the app, Apple's rather small modifications to PDFs in Apple Notes turn out to be more substantial than they might first appear to be.


***Add more than one PDF to a note:***

- Choose an existing note or create a new one.
- Drag a PDF file into it.
- then add a new PDF to it.


You are free to keep adding PDFs as you choose, and you probably will now that they are displayed in such a much better way. Even though macOS Sonoma is still in beta, it does appear to take longer to drag in a PDF and make it legible. It's also possible that you may now open the PDF in Apple Notes and read every page of it there. Apple Notes is therefore displaying a picture of all the pages, not just the first.


The PDF no longer only shows the first page to make sure you can't miss what it's changed. Instead, a page from the center of the document is displayed, along with some of the pages before and following it. The exact location depends on the PDF's page count.


The PDF that is embedded can no longer be opened in another program by clicking on it. You must use the Share option when you right-click on the PDF if you still want to do that. However, since you can now view the entire PDF in one spot, there is minimal need. The fact that you have to swipe to open the first page is a tad tiresome, though.

The new option has replaced the outdated "View as Small Images" option, and it is superior. Show Thumbnails is the new selection. It is a button in the upper right corner of the PDF page you are now viewing, and it only relates to that particular PDF.

Therefore, if you click it, a row of thumbnails appears at the top along with the fully legible PDF page that was previously displayed. You may swipe more rapidly to any page by clicking in that row.

Additionally, none of the other PDFs in the letter are impacted as you do this to one of them. If you choose, you may drag a thumbnail page out of the note, which creates a single-page PDF document wherever you drop it. Unfortunately, it currently appears that exporting the entire PDF will not be as simple.

**New view option**

Apple does make it quite apparent that you may now read a PDF in its whole, but other capabilities, like as how you can view that document specifically, are more unclear.

In Notes, PDFs are shown embedded in a light gray box with the filename of the document and an ellipses icon in the upper left corner. In addition to what was previously available in the right-click popup menu, such as Markup, clicking that brings up a new view choice.

You have the choice of Large, Medium, or Small for that attachment display, in that order. Once more, the decision you make here just affects the PDF that is now chosen, not all of the PDFs in a note.

It also implies that, in principle, you may set up the view such that you can view and read two PDFs side by side for comparison. In actuality, it depends on the nature of the PDFs; for example, text with a lot of density might not look its best in the Medium view. However, the ability to read a PDF in its entirety at full screen width, or alternatively reduced, is revolutionary. It's unfortunate that the Markup tool is once more hidden away; it's puzzling why it isn't just accessible from the right-click menu.

Even though this version of macOS Sonoma is still in beta, it seems doubtful that Apple would add the Markup tool to the right-click menu or even make it more apparent than it now is. It appears that the business has had it buried behind a little down arrow for long time since it is not a top concern.

### Form filling

However, Markup is now more significant. Apple also highlighted the fact that macOS Sonoma can now recognize when a PDF is actually a form, but neglected to explain that this requires Markup. Rather, it does so when Apple Notes is open and the PDF is present. Simply opening a PDF in Preview will let you to see where you need to fill out a form's box, and macOS Sonoma has already made that location clickable.

It works the same way in Apple Notes, except that you can only click on a text field on a form after you've selected to utilize Markup. Although not a significant additional step, it is somewhat obscured.

## Fill Out Documents Faster With Autofill

Users may now download the public beta of macOS Sonoma, which offers consumers intriguing capabilities for document management. "Document AutoFill," which makes it easier to fill out PDF fields, is one feature that stands out.

Many people have always found it difficult to fill out PDF forms, but macOS Sonoma solves this problem and makes it simple. The general comfort it gives when working on a Mac is a significant benefit of readily filling out PDF data.

### Using Document AutoFill

Employing Document A uncomplicated procedure, AutoFill may be finished in only two easy steps:

- Launch the chosen PDF file.
- Fill in the fields by clicking the Document AutoFill button in the top right corner.

We discovered that changing the font or text size is not currently feasible in the Public Beta version. The typed text, however, is usable right away. We anticipate that the complete macOS 14 or macOS Sonoma releases will include more choices for adjusting this functionality. (Note: Try it out on iOS 17 and iPadOS 17 as well; this functionality is supported in both of those operating systems' Public Beta releases.)

**Supported Mac Models for macOS Sonoma**

- iMac Pro (2017 and later)

- Mac Pro (2019 and later)

- MacBook Air (2018 and later)

- MacBook Pro (2018 and later)

- iMac (2019 and later)

- Mac mini (2018 and later)

- Mac Studio (2022 and later)

(Please take note that this new content has been edited for grammar and is written in a formal, professional tone.) OS X Sonoma Using Document AutoFill to fill out PDF forms is simple.This use will definitely please the document line!

**macOS Sonoma Fill out PDF data easily, along with Document AutoFill.**

General users may now download the public beta version of macOS Sonoma. The "Document AutoFill" option is one of the intriguing tools that will probably fulfill your demands when dealing with papers. With the help of this function, we can easily fill up the fields in the PDF document, which is typically a hassle for many individuals. Having said that, working on a Mac is quite pleasant due to the fact that we can simply fill in PDF data.

**How to use Document AutoFill**

***How to use Document AutoFill is very simple, in 2 steps:***

1. Let's start by opening the appropriate PDF file.
2. You may fill up the blanks by clicking the Document AutoFill feature button in the top right corner.

## LINK RELATED NOTES

You can provide a link to join similar remarks in macOS Sonoma. You might, for instance, connect a list of suggested eateries to a vacation plan. Please take note that older macOS devices may not display notes that include links to other notes. Please go to Why notes are buried on some devices.

- Select Edit > Add Link in your Mac's Notes application.

- Enter a note's title here. A list of notes that match what you're typing emerges.

- Select a note.

- To always have the link text match the title of the linked note, choose Use Note Title. To change the link's wording, deselect the checkbox.

- Select OK.

**Tip:** Type the greater than symbol twice (>>) to rapidly link to another note. The link title always reflects the current title of the note it connects to when you use this shortcut.

## START IN NOTES AND FINISH IN PAGES

Apple Notes is a full-featured note-taking tool in many aspects. It allows you to take notes, make to-do lists, schedule your day, and much more thanks to its extensive selection of simple-to-use features. However, the Apple Notes app doesn't have the word processing features you'll need to produce papers with a professional appearance. And for that reason, it's a pleasant convenience that Apple Notes may now be converted into Pages documents in iOS 17 and macOS 14 Sonoma. In particular for those who extensively rely on these two well-known Apple programs for writing or developing projects.

### TURN APPLE NOTES INTO PAGES DOCUMENTS ON MAC

*It's as straightforward to turn a particular note into a Pages document.*

- Open the Notes program on your Mac to get started.

- Find the note you want to open in the Pages app by navigating there.

- Next, click the Share button in the interface's top right corner.

- After that, just select "Open in Pages" and you're done!

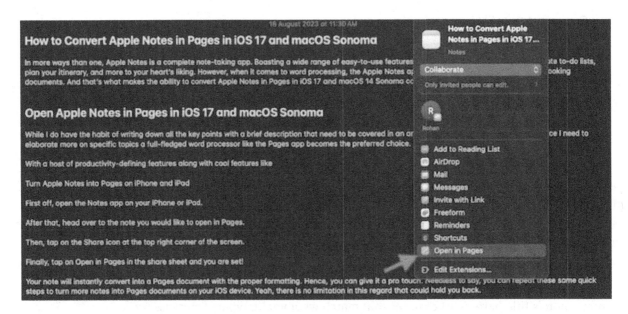

The seamless experience is what sets the Apple ecosystem apart from the competition. This most recent feature, as far as I can tell, is an example of it.

# KEYBOARD

The keyboard will change, including enhanced Autocorrect and typing predictions. Your train of thought won't be interrupted by using the keyboard and dictation simultaneously in macOS Sonoma. In other words, after pressing the Dictation shortcut (assignable in System Settings -> Keyboard), you can continue typing. Therefore, if your fingers need a break, you may finish the statement by speaking it aloud.

# PRIVACY AND SECURITY

Every year, Apple highlights aspects that people will find fascinating when it unveils its newest operating systems. Operating systems this year provide options like iPad lock screen personalization, Mac screensavers, and stickers for usage in Messages. However, Apple also includes fresh privacy and security measures in every update to its operating systems. The new security and privacy features in iOS 17, iPadOS 17, and macOS Sonoma are summarized here.

## COMMUNICATION SAFETY

- **Safari**

One of the essential components for ensuring users of computer devices have both security and privacy is the web browser. It serves as a portal to the Internet and serves as the primary entry point for fraudsters looking to compromise your devices. Additionally, websites make an effort to gather personal information about you by tracking your surfing patterns and history.

Apple has updated Safari to include certain security and privacy enhancements across all of its operating systems. The first is profiles, which enable you establish various Safari profiles, for example, for usage at work and at home. Every profile has its own history, extensions, tab groups, cookies, and favorite items. When using your personal profile, you could have more privacy protection than your workplace permits. Alternately, your employer can decide to have tighter security and permit fewer extensions.

The privacy of browsing is being improved. Since they are now closed when you utilize private or browsing windows and turn your Mac off, no one can see what you were looking at. You must authenticate with a password, Touch ID, or Face ID in order to see these windows. In addition to blocking known trackers altogether from loading on pages, private browsing also deletes tracking that is added to URLs as you browse.

**Private Browsing Is Locked**

Touch ID or enter the password for the user
"Kirk McElhearn" to view these tabs.

Enter password

### Passwords and passkeys

Although passwords and passkeys are extremely private, there are numerous situations where sharing them is desirable. For certain services, your family members may use the same account, or at work, your entire team may use shared passwords to access particular websites.

One issue with this is that you have to inform everyone of the new passwords whenever you need to change them. With the ability to form a group, you may share passwords and passkeys with others, and their iCloud Keychain will always include the most recent versions of these credentials.

### Two-factor authentication

Wherever it is practical, you should always utilize two-factor authentication. Many websites only utilize the basic kind of two-factor authentication (2FA), which includes sending you a six-digit number through email or text message. Six-digit 2FA codes that receive through text message are already auto-filled in Safari. Safari will also automatically enter these codes if they are sent by email on the operating systems of this year. Additionally, after the text messages containing these codes have been filled in, Messages will immediately erase them.

### Lockdown Mode

A formidable feature in macOS, iOS, and iPadOS, as well as one that will soon be available for watchOS, called Lockdown Mode, strengthens the security of your devices to fend off potential targeted assaults. Lockdown mode for the Mac, iPhone, iPad, and for the first time ever, the Apple Watch will be useful for individuals in critical positions even if the majority of people don't require it.

**Lockdown Mode**

Lockdown Mode is an extreme, optional protection that should only be used if you believe you may be personally targeted by a highly sophisticated cyberattack. Most people are never targeted by attacks of this nature.

For complete protection, Lockdown Mode has to be enabled on all your devices. Apps, websites, and features will be strictly limited for security, and some experiences will be completely unavailable.

Learn more...

Turn On Lockdown Mode

Sensitive content protection

When sensitive videos or photographs are received, Communication Safety warns users so they are not exposed to them. It will be expanded to cover content shared and received via AirDrop, the system-wide photo picker, FaceTime messaging, Contact Posters in the Phone app, and third-party applications. Previously, it was only accessible in messaging.

Additionally, you will be able to blur private images and videos before choosing to view them in third-party applications, FaceTime messaging, AirDrop, Contact Posters in the Phone app, and messaging.

**Apple ID**

You utilize Apple's two-factor authentication when you need to sign into a new Apple device or use an Apple service for the first time. Other devices you own receive authentication tokens from Apple. However, you will also be able to transmit authentication codes to anybody nearby with an Apple device, as well as to anyone whose email address or phone number is listed in your Apple ID account. You may set up trusted phone numbers for anyone who can receive these codes.

## Additional privacy features

To grant or deny an app access to the camera, microphone, or specific areas on a Mac where data are kept, there are already a lot of granular permissions choices in all of Apple's operating systems. These permissions also include the ability to share a photo without giving the app access to your full photo collection or to add an event to your calendar without giving the app access to your other calendar information.

## New AirTag feature

Apple will enable the sharing of AirTags, resolving a privacy concern with these trackers. All AirTags are now associated with unique Apple IDs, but Apple will soon let up to five persons to track AirTags. This may be helpful, for example, if someone attached an AirTag to a shared bicycle or if two individuals alternately use a bag when traveling. Alternatively, if two individuals are traveling together and one or both of them has an AirTag on their keys, they could both receive notifications that read, "AirTag Found Moving With You." Each user will stop receiving notifications if they add the AirTag to their accounts.

Cancel

# Share This AirTag

**Car Keys**
You're the owner

WHAT WILL HAPPEN

**Others can locate this AirTag**
Everyone who shares this AirTag can locate it in Find My.

**Tracking notifications will be muted**
Everyone who shares this AirTag won't get notified when it's near them.

All persons who have access to shared AirTags will be able to follow those who are wearing them. In order to track their children, parents may attach AirTags to their children's keys. However, if two parents shared AirTags on their keys, they could also track one another. The aforementioned new capabilities will be included in the upcoming autumn releases of macOS Sonoma, iOS 17, and iPadOS 17.

# SENSITIVE CONTENT WARNING

The ability to share photographs and movies is a convenience that comes with your Mac computer. You never know when you'll share or get anything offensive, though. You may use macOS Sonoma's Sensitive Content Warning to stay away from such possibilities. In order to enable Sensitive Content Warning on Mac running macOS Sonoma & later, follow this instruction whether you're a worried parent or appreciate a more mindful surfing experience.

Use the macOS Sonoma sensitive content warning feature by turning it on. Before continuing, let's have a thorough discussion of this new function and grasp its many facets.

## What does the macOS Sonoma "Sensitive Content Warning" mean?

The communication Safety feature that attempts to prevent you and your children from accessing sensitive Content like inappropriate images and videos, receiving through FaceTime Message, AirDrop, iMessage, etc. has been expanded by the privacy and security feature known as "Sensitive Content Warning."

## How Does Sensitive Content Warning Work?

When this feature is enabled, the Mac employs on-device machine learning to check for the Content that needs to be reported each time it receives hazardous content from the supported apps. The content will get obscured or hidden if any graphic or violent images are found.

## What happens if a user attempts to access Content while the warning is active?

When you attempt to access sensitive Content again, you will be informed of this. Three alternatives are available on the warning page, Not Now, I'm sure of the ways to get help.

Not Now: If you don't wish to access the Content, choose this option.

Ways to Get Help: If sensitive Content has been shared with you without your authorization, this choice will direct you to the tools and links you may use to get assistance.

I'm sure: If you wish to view the received Content while skipping the warning, use this option.

## Which Apps Support Sensitive Content Warnings?

Apple apps and services are the only ones that now provide the Sensitive Content Warning feature. Apple has, however, also made it available to third-party programs. Therefore, we accept the apps listed below.

- AirDrop.
- Apple Messages.
- Third-party Apps.

**What Type of Content Can Get a Sensitive Content Warning?**

Any image or video that contains degrading material will be labeled as "Sensitive Content," including degrading images and videos, screenshots, and damaging memes.

**What About the Privacy of the Photos/Videos, and Do Apple Have Access to Them?**

The major question now Can I trust the sensitive content warning? Does Apple have access to pictures and videos? The good news is that Apple has created obscene Content detection technology for on-device video/image processing. It indicates that neither the firm nor any third parties will have access to your data. As a result, using the function on your Mac is secure.

**How to make macOS Sonoma's sensitive content warning functional**

Now that you are aware of the "Sensitive Content Warning," here are detailed instructions on turning it on in macOS Sonoma.

Keep in mind that macOS 14 introduces this functionality. Therefore, read our post on updating your Mac if you haven't done so already.

- Click the Apple Logo. Select System Settings...
- In the left pane, select Privacy & Security.
- Click on the Sensitive Content Warning link on the right.

- Switch on the Sensitive Content Warning toggle.
- After you enable the feature, the supported applications and services that support it will be listed below App & Service Access. To apply the Sensitive Content Warning, just tap the toggle next to the app.

- You may also choose to Improve Sensitive Content Warning. Your messages or data will be examined and shared with Apple if you turn it on. If you wish to keep your data entirely anonymous, switch off this function, which is optional.

**How to Deal with the Content that has been flagged as Sensitive**

You will be given the opportunity to take additional action if any of your Content is determined to be sensitive.

**Show:** You may view the Content by clicking the Show button.

**Warning Icon:** by clicking the Warning Icon to provide two choices.

**Ways To Get Help:** By selecting this option, you will be sent to the Apple Support website, where you may find a variety of information to help you make the best decision.

**Block Contact:** It will block the contact.

Advice for selecting which Content has to be designated as sensitive

Sensitive anything Warning, a new feature from Apple, flags anything that can be sexually explicit or provocative, such as images, graphic depictions, or memes of individuals wearing transparent clothes.

Thanks to Apple, who regularly improves consumer privacy. If your child uses a Mac, the sensitive material warning function not only spares you the humiliation but also stops them from sharing or receiving such material.

## LOCKDOWN MODE

With every software update, Apple puts privacy and security first. Apple has made Lockdown Mode, a feature that aids users in staying safe, available with macOS Ventura.

Remember that your Mac machine is running macOS Sonoma while you read this information regarding Lockdown Mode and how to use it.

### What is Lockdown Mode?

Lockdown mode, as the name implies, effectively locks down your Mac machine from a security perspective. By restricting key features on your Mac, such as receiving the majority of iMessage attachments, barring specific web technologies, and even banning FaceTime calls from ominous callers, it strengthens security to defend against cyberattacks.

Additionally, you are unable to unlock your Mac and accept any physical peripheral connections. The nicest aspect of this capability is that you can activate Apple Watch as well as any other Apple accessories.

### What Impact Does the Lockdown Mode Have on Your Device?

Apple claims that once you activate lockdown mode on your Mac device, a number of factors start to work against you. The modifications you'll notice after activating Lockdown mode on your Mac are listed below.

### Messages

- Other picture types and attachments are blocked.
- The link previews are turned off.

**Apple Service**

- Incoming invites and service requests are disabled, and FaceTime calls are also blocked.

**Web Browser**

Unless you remove the trusted sites from Lockdown mode, web technologies like JIT compilation and other services are disabled. All of these limitations are applied to Safari and other WebKit-based browsers.

**Other**

When a Mac computer or accessory is locked, all physical connections to the device are barred.

**How to Turn on the Lockdown Mode on Mac**

The privacy of high-risk customers is safeguarded by the lockdown mode, which serves as a defense or security mechanism against extremely sophisticated cyberattacks. Because it prevents some websites, functions, and applications from operating on your device because of the vulnerability of the data being utilized by the websites, the majority of users might not even sense the need to enable this mode. Therefore, if you belong to one of the high-risk user groups, such as journalists or activists, and want to activate the lockdown mode on your Mac, refer to the steps listed below.

**Step 1:** To begin, click on the Apple logo at the top to open the system settings box.

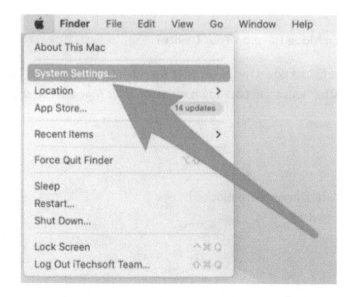

**Step 2:** In the system settings box, select the "Security & Privacy" tab.

**Step 3:** Navigate to "Lockdown Mode"

**Step 4:** To activate the lockdown mode on your MacBook, click the "Turn On..." button. Use Touch ID for verification now, or your Mac's login password, to turn it on.

**Step 5:** choose Turn on & Restart. This means that when your Mac is in Lockdown Mode, several functionality, programs, and websites are severely restricted for security reasons.

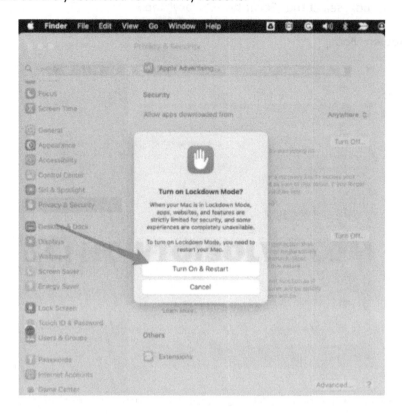

That's it! You may use this to activate lockdown mode on your MacBook, but many functions, programs, and websites won't be available. Therefore, you should enable this mode if you work as a journalist, activist, or in any other job where you run the danger of being targeted by cyberterrorists or hackers. But before turning on lockdown mode on their MacBook, everyone else should exercise extreme caution.

# CONCLUSION

These days, MacBooks are among the most feature-rich laptops available, despite their high price. In spite of their expensive cost. If you're unfamiliar with the macOS environment, trying to get a hold of your new laptop may seem incredibly daunting. Since the introduction of macOS 13 Ventura, which offers a plethora of fascinating and inventive features, the MacBook Air has become the best laptop on the market.

Whether you got your MacBook as a gift or purchased it for yourself as a treat for work, school, or a passion project, this book is the best choice if you want to make the most of it.

This user manual for Mac only covers a small portion of the accessible topics. As you use your Mac more often, you'll discover more about its capabilities. The best advice I can offer you is to just enjoy using your Mac since there are a ton of other options.

## DO NOT GO YET; ONE LAST THING TO DO

I would really appreciate it if you could leave a brief Amazon review if you liked the book or found it helpful. Your encouragement does matter, and I personally read every review to obtain your thoughts and improve this book.

Once again, I appreciate your help!

# INDEX

Made in the USA
Las Vegas, NV
20 May 2024

90154875R00072